My Church My Family

How to Have a Healthy Relationship with the Church

by: Dr. James B. Richards

Impact Ministries
Publications Department
3516 South Broad Place
Huntsville, AL 35805
(205)536-9402 or (205)536-2633

(Not affiliated with Impact Publishers, Inc.
San Luis Obispo, California.)

Impact Ministries
Publications Department
3516 South Broad Place
Huntsville, AL 35805
(205)536-9402 or (205)536-2633
Fax: (205)536-4530

Table of Contents

Read This First

The end does not justify the means, but it does determine the means. The destination does determine the direction. When you decide to take a trip, you do not try to determine your route first. You must first decide your destination. The destination is the single-most essential factor in determining the route that will be chosen. If I decide to take a vacation in a particular city in the United States, I then need a map of the United States. Every journey begins with deciding the destination and acquiring the proper map. Without both, you will surely lose your way.

No amount of effort, "faith" or determination will cause me to reach the proper destination if I have the wrong map. Also, the proper map will not help me if I do not know the destination. How we interpret God's intentions for man determines our understanding of the destination or goal that we should pursue. Our understanding of the goal determines how we will map our life and where we will spend our energies.

Your understanding of the goal creates your paradigm, your life-dominating concepts. Your paradigm determines your perspective. From your perspective, you see things a certain way; you evaluate, interpret, plan and determine priority. If your paradigm (concept of God's goal) is improper, you will have wrong priorities. You will have the wrong map. Your efforts may be genuine and diligent, but you will never reach the proper destination.

I believe most Christians are sincere. I think most Christians desire to live a life pleasing to God. The problem is we have accepted the wrong destination; we are using the wrong map. Churches spend billions of dollars, millions of man hours and untold amounts of energy pursuing the wrong goals.

One day, I returned to my hotel room after speaking in a morning session. My wife had been watching one of the most popular ministers in America. She was so distraught at the absence of logic, practicality, relevance and reality that he was preaching. Thousands of people were hanging on his every word as he explained how God had established marriage for *spiritual warfare*. What a distorted paradigm. If that is what he really believes about marriage, I feel sorry for his wife and children.

Because he has the wrong destination in mind, he will use the wrong map. Every day he will put forth effort to reach that destination. When he reaches that destination, he will probably have to deal with a divorce. Spiritual warfare is not the reason God instituted marriage. He said, *"It is not good for man to be alone."* Genesis 2:18. God created marriage for companionship, and companionship is expressed through relationship.

All of this man's efforts will destroy intimacy, self-worth, and trust in his relationship. When he sees the problems emerge he may work his plan even harder, but that will only make the problems worse. Because of his paradigm, he will never see that he is working the wrong plan. He will blame it on his wife, his children, or some unseen mystical force. His map has taken him to a destination that will not provide what he expects.

Similarly, our paradigm of the church has brought as much destruction as anything I know. The church is the number one reason for the way the world views God. We have caused the world to not want our God nor His wisdom. We have misrepresented God to the world. The church is preached as an army, a hospital, a factory, a convention center, a teaching seminar, an evangelistic outreach and a thousand other misconceptions. While the church may be involved in all these aspects, none of these tell us what the church really is. The church is not an army; it is a family. We are not here to *attack* the world with the *power* of God; we are here to **win** the world with the *love* of God.

Jesus came to bring us into the family of God. More than anything else, we are God's children. Children thrive in loving, family relationships.   In a family there is teaching, adoption (evangelism), and many other aspects of family life, but more than anything else, there is relationship.   There is love, trust, friendship, growing together, working together, and playing together.

The church is here to meet the greatest, emotional need in a person's life: relationship. Because our paradigm has been wrong, the leaders have not offered a family, and the members have not sought to build a family. That is why there are millions of people worldwide who are hurt and disillusioned with the church. People are leaving by the thousands each year.

The answer is not to reject the church; the answer is to transform it. We, as members, need to reject unscriptural paradigms about the church and God. We need to put our efforts into the things that the Bible clearly prioritizes. We should lovingly refuse to allow leaders to turn us into an army. We are a family and it is time we begin to live like a family.

Your life will be totally transformed when you learn to have a healthy relationship with a church.   You will find the peace, security, friendship and joy that can only come from meaningful, healthy relationships with your brothers and sisters in the family of God.

Chapter 1

Healthy Relationships

One of the greatest paradoxes of life is the source of pain and pleasure. Whatever has the potential to bring the most pleasure always has the potential to bring us the greatest amount of pain, if mishandled. Therefore, we must face and conquer what we fear, and often what has brought us the greatest pain, in order to find the greatest fulfillment.

This principle is seen most clearly in the arena of relationships. We are emotional, social, relationship-oriented beings. It is a part of our makeup to need healthy relationships. We cannot become what we should be, apart from meaningful relationships. Yet, abusive relationships are the single greatest source of pain in our life. Therefore, we have become a society devoid of commitment to relationships. We have withdrawn from the pursuit of relationships in the fear of being hurt. In the vacuum of isolation, we occasionally break out and try again, but because our ideas about relationships are the same as before, we experience the same hurts and disappointments.

The source of all of our hurt is not relationships. The pain is the result of the pursuit of relationships apart from the principles of God. God's Word clearly lays out all of the principles we will ever need to build worthwhile relationships while avoiding hurt. A failure to observe and embrace these principles always results in destroyed relationships and heartache.

God's Word is very clear about the type of people that we should allow as a source of fellowship. The people with whom we fellowship will influence us more than the people who teach us. They will influence us more than those who have brought us to Jesus. Our friends will affect our beliefs and attitudes more than those who have ministered to us, served us, brought us deliverance and interceded for us.

For this reason, the Bible is very clear about the kind of people with whom we should associate. "*He that walketh with wise men shall be wise: but a companion of fools shall be destroyed.*" Proverbs 13:20. We will become like our friends. We will have victory from their victories—or we will develop their attitudes, suffer from their emotional wounds, and assume their offenses.

The Book of Hebrews exhorts us to, ". . . *follow those who by faith and patience inherit the promises.*" Hebrews 6:12. The reality is, we will inherit whatever the people have that are influencing us. If they are in strife, we will be in strife. If they are critical, we will be critical. Their enemies will become our enemies and their friends will become our friends. The end of their ways will be the end of our ways.

Despite how much a person meets a need in my life, I must look at what they are experiencing in their own life before I can decide if I will allow them to speak into my life. It is often hard to see the real picture of someone's life in our society. There are many ways to mask reality. It usually takes a great deal of time before we really see the fruit of someone's life. As Paul warned Timothy, *"Some men's sins are open beforehand, going before to judgment; and some men they follow after."* 1 Timothy 5:24.

This does not necessitate that we live in fear about every relationship. It does, however, mean that we should use a great deal of wisdom and caution. Proverbs 12:26 in the NIV says, *"A wise man is cautious in friendship . . ."* Caution should not be the product of fear; it should be the product of wisdom. As the saying goes, "Fools rush in where wise men fear to tread." A wise person uses caution and weighs the risks in every area of life, including friendship.

Every parent cautions their child about the friends that he selects. We all know that peer pressure is one of the greatest forces in character development. 1 Corinthians 15:33 in the NIV warns, *"Do not be mislead: Bad company corrupts good character."* While we are quick to realize this with our children, we assume that we are too smart to let that happen to us. We get involved with people who have negative attitudes, walk in sin, or have bad character and then think it will not affect us. The truth applies whether we are age five or 50. We are influenced by the friends we select.

Out of our God-given desire to have friends, we often spurn the wisdom of God's Word and rush into friendships unwisely and suffer the painful consequences. We want to have friends that believe in us. We want to hear people tell us we are right. Out of this need, we often make ourselves vulnerable at the most inappropriate times. At times when God may be challenging us about gossip, strife or other destructive attitudes, the last thing we need is for someone to come along and tell us it is all right.

Leaders have falsely assumed that if people believe in us, we will have the power to influence them. The opposite, however, is nearer to the truth. It is the people who believe *in me* that I will allow to influence me the most, not the ones I believe in. As *laymen* we are not sure that our leaders believe in us, but we do think that our friends believe in us. We think that when they go along with us, they are really for us. This is not the Bible perspective. "*A man that flattereth his neighbour spreadeth a net for his feet."* Proverbs 29:5. A real friend will always challenge our sinful attitudes and encourage us in the pursuit of truth.

Because leaders often play a role in us facing some of the most challenging and difficult issues of our life, there is much room for offense against the leader. Many times the leader who helps us face an issue, becomes the blame for the pain. At that time, we will often look for those who will console us and take our position. That person is not the friend we assume. *"A lying tongue hateth those that are afflicted by it; and a flattering mouth worketh ruin."* Proverbs 26:28.

At this vulnerable time, we abandon those who love us for those who will agree with us. We fall into a trap of unhealthy relationships that forever alters the course of our life. There are, of course, hundreds of other scenarios why we abandon our church, friends and leaders who love us and watch for our souls. We walk down a pathway that seems right, but in the end is more pain. *"There is a way which seemeth right unto a man, but the end thereof are the ways of death. Even in laughter the heart is sorrowful; and the end of that mirth is heaviness."* Proverbs 14:13.

There will be flaws in every church. There will be some situations that require you to make a change in churches. But there is *never* any excuse for one to abandon the local church.

If we manage our relationships with the people and the leadership according to Biblical principles, we can never be abused. There can be disappointments, there can be problems, but the benefits of a healthy relationship with a church far outweigh the disadvantages.

All healthy relationships require effort, planning, and godly wisdom. If we abandon the principles of healthy relationships found in the Word of God, we will suffer for it. We will have bad experiences no matter where we go. But there is a way to have healthy relationships with those who are walking with God. There is a way to be committed without crossing the line of co-dependence. There is a way to make sacrifices and not be consumed. All of this lies within *us*. It is not determined by the motives or actions of others, it is determined by our own heart.

At a time when people are screaming "church abuse," we may need to look in the mirror and shout, "Scriptural neglect!" Even when leaders are abusive, it is my neglect of scriptural truth that allows the abuse in my life. I will not reject the church because of the problems. The church is the only organization that Jesus came to establish. I need the church and the church needs me. It is time that I stop being naive and acting as a child. Then I will have the meaningful, healthy relationships that I need for my life.

Chapter 2

The Need for a Church

Although you never find the phrase *church membership* in the New Testament, you do find a much stronger phrase that describes an individual's relationship with the local church. The Bible says in the Book of Acts, *". . . souls were added to the church . . ."* The soul of a man is his emotional being. It is the place of his logical mind, emotions and will: his ability to make willful decisions and commitments.

In the early church they did not have their name on roll sheets. Something happened to them that made them have an emotional attachment, a willful commitment and a logical realization of their need for the church body. They were added to the Body of Christ (the worldwide church) by being born again. But they were added to the local church *emotionally* as a response to the ministry they had received. They knew they needed the church. What happened in them was far more powerful than signing their name to a roll sheet.

Becoming an official member of a local church should follow receiving ministry. Many people attend one church as an obligation and receive ministry from other churches. That is not healthy. It is fine and healthy to receive ministry from other churches, but ultimately we will have no value for a place where we are not receiving meaningful ministry. We cannot respond properly to something that adds nothing to our lives.

When we are receiving ministry that adds to our lives, it produces a healthy response of commitment and relationship. We have an appreciation and attachment because of receiving ministry. One should only become a member of a church because they have an attachment. There should be a heartfelt relationship with your church of choice. Anything less is of no real value.

Throughout history the local church has met many important needs for God's people. The early believers recognized that it was essential to identify with and be a part of a local church. They knew they would not survive without the support, friendship, encouragement and teaching of the local church. People relating to one another in groups has been the pattern God has used since the beginning. As Genesis 2:18 says, *"It is not good for man to dwell alone."*

Man was created to be in relationships. We are not designed to dwell alone. That is why God created marriage, the family and the congregation. When man is left to himself, the end is seldom good. The church meets an essential need in a person's life that will never be met if he dwells alone.

The Bible says, *"Two are better than one, because they have a good return for their work: If one falls down, his friend can help him up. But pity the man who falls and has no one to help him up! Also, if two lie down together, they will keep warm. But how can one keep warm alone? Though one may be overpowered, two can defend themselves. A cord of three strands is not easily broken."* Ecclesiastes 4:9-12 NIV. Throughout both the Old and New Testaments there is continual reference to the congregation. God has always had the intention that His people be a group which works and flows together. For that reason, we are described as a family, a body, citizens, a congregation, etc.

While we relate to God individually, we become a part of a group. This group, called the church, functions together to accomplish the will of God in the earth. We minister to one another and reach the world. We protect and care for one another. We become a part of an extended family that grows in relationships. It is through our relationships with people that our Christianity is developed. Our involvement with people is where our love for God is reflected, expressed and often experienced. (1 John 4)

Jesus described the church as His body. In

the Book of Corinthians, Paul continued this analogy. The parts of the body cannot survive alone and even if they could, they could not function or be of any real value if they were alone. Similarly, as part of the body of Christ, we need one another. We need the strength that comes from being a part of a healthy body. We need one another. Through our shortsightedness we fail to fully understand our need for one another. But be assured, Paul was speaking by the Spirit of God when he said, *"And whether one member suffer, all the members suffer . . ."* 1 Corinthians 12:26.

In his early missionary journeys, the Apostle Paul established churches and ordained elders in every city. He knew that people would not survive if left on their own. Corinthians says that the Old Testament serves as an example to us and one of the greatest examples we have of our need for the body was when Israel was without leaders. The Book of Judges clearly records the up-down, on-off relationship that Israel had with God. They would forget God, get into trouble, get into bondage, then finally call out to God and He would deliver them. They would return to God for a season, only to forget Him again as their troubles dissipated. They went through this cycle many times. This confusing, difficult time was the product of a particular attitude that existed during that time. *"Every man did that which was right in his own eyes. "* Judges 17:6.

We do not have to learn by going through the pain of a "roller coaster" life. We can follow the teaching presented in the Word of God and have victory and stability. The following chapters will help you understand the value of being a part of a local church and help you recognize the signs of a healthy church. They will also help you avoid abusive and destructive church involvement.

It takes time and effort to cultivate an emotional relationship with a church. It also takes the realization of the need. Like the children of Israel who wandered through the wilderness, we need one another. Like the early church, we will not survive and become whole if we abide alone.

Chapter 3

A Place of Healing

The church should be a place of healing as much as anything. While physical healing is important and scriptural, it is not the greatest need in your life. Emotional needs are more spiritually limiting than physical needs. Until a person is made whole emotionally, he cannot enter into meaningful relationships with God or people.

In more than twenty years of ministry, the most common limiting factor I have seen is rejection. Rejection takes place when a person is unable to give and receive love. No matter how much one person loves another, if rejection is present it will never be realized. Rejected people do not feel loved. When people *do* show them love, they do not have the capacity to receive it.

God created us to know Him and experience His wonderful love. He desired a relationship with man from the beginning. If we are incapable of entering into that relationship, we have missed the primary purpose for our existence. Apart from experiencing the love of God, we will never be made whole. Our life will always be empty. We will always have an unfulfilled longing.

Just as rejection (the inability to give and receive love) affects our relationships with people, it also affects our relationship with God. How we relate to people is a mirror of how we relate to God. We have many of the same difficulties in relating to God that we have in relating to people. Although God did not inflict the hurts and pains in our lives, just as pain limits our relationships with people, it also limits our relationship with God.

Jesus came to set the captives free. The captives are those people who are held captive because of the sins, hurts, wounds, and shame that had been inflicted upon them and by them. The captives are those whose hearts have been broken by the experiences of life. When Jesus arrived on the scene He said, *"The Spirit of the Lord is upon me, because he hath anointed me to preach the gospel to the poor; he hath sent me to heal the brokenhearted, to preach deliverance to the captives, and recovering of sight to the blind, to set at liberty them that are bruised."* Luke 4:18.

Jesus came to set us free from the captivities of this life. He came to set us free from sin and its effects. He came to make us whole so we could have a relationship with God the Father. He said, *"And this is life eternal, that they might know thee the only true God, and Jesus Christ, whom thou hast sent. He came to restore us to God."* John 17:3.

It is the goal of God that every believer enters into meaningful relationships with Him and with others. He is our Father. We are His children. We are a part of the family of God. We were created for the sole purpose of knowing and fellowshipping with God. We are the objects of His love and affection. Until we are made whole, we will not have the capacity to receive and experience the love God has for us. What we *do for* God is secondary to having a relationship *with* Him.

Jesus gave the fivefold ministry as a gift to the church. It is the job of the apostles, prophets, evangelists, pastors and teachers to *". . . perfect the saints for the work of the ministry . . ."* Ephesians 4:12.

The word *perfect* comes from a Greek word whose root meaning is "to mend or make whole." Through the ministry of the Word, personal example and meaningful relationships, people are healed from the wounds and hurts that have been inflicted upon them. They are made whole to enable them to have meaningful relationships with God and people.

It should be our goal as the church to teach and exemplify the love of God. We should build a Bible-based sense of self-worth that will cause you to grasp the great love and value God has for you. As this happens, you will be freed from the limitations you have placed on your life. You will be free to have meaningful relationships. You will be free to fulfill the purpose of God for your life.

We must realize, this ministry of making people whole was specifically given to the fivefold ministry.   To sever ourselves from meaningful ministry is to sever ourselves from the very instruments sent to bring us to a place of wholeness.

The believer must use discretion in selecting a church. We must discover if it is the goal of the minister to help us find wholeness. We choose whom we will subject ourselves to, and we must make that choice wisely.

We cannot use the failings and wrong motives of some to justify not having meaningful relations with the church. We need the ministry gifts of the fivefold minster. This gift will be part of the process by which we find wholeness.

Chapter 4

Relationships: The Place of Perfection

There is no greater need in a person's life than that of meaningful relationships, yet there is nothing more threatening. We were created in the likeness and image of God and He is a social, emotional, relationship-oriented being. From the beginning He said, *"It is not good that the man should be alone."* Genesis 2:18.

From the first breath of mankind until now, our needs for social and relationship skills have grown. At first it was easy; Adam simply related to a perfect God. Relating to someone who is perfect presents no real challenges. From there, Adam had to learn to relate to a wife and then children. Then came families, cities, nations and ultimately the world. When Jesus came, He established the church, which should become the hub of our relationships as Christians. Other Christians are the only source of true fellowship we have in this world.

Jesus was the friend of sinners, yet His involvement with sinners always revolved around the fact that He was ministering to them.

Similarly, we should have the ability to befriend the lost, but we must realize that when sinners become our source of fellowship (when our involvement no longer has ministry as its goal) we are headed for trouble. Psychologists have verified that if a person receives treatment, improves and then goes back into the same environment, they will seldom maintain the level of progress they have made. Similarly, the Christian who looks to the lost, backslidden or rebellious for fellowship will not remain stable.

This principle is clear throughout the Bible. In the Old Testament God called the people out. In 2 Corinthians 6:17, Paul is warning about fellowship with the world as he instructs, "*Wherefore come out from among them, and be ye separate, saith the Lord . . .*" When people fail to be involved with the church on a social level, it is only a matter of time before they backslide. Of all the things that may concern me in a person's life, this is one of the greatest indicators of an eminent fall.

It is no different from when a person stops having particular emotional needs met by their mate. If they begin to spend time with someone else to meet those needs, it is only a matter of time before there is a divorce. With whom we spend time indicates more about where we are going than almost any other factor.

Very early in my walk with God I realized

the value of Christian fellowship. I saw that I could not make it if I did not establish strong ties in the church. Most of the people I know who were saved at that time are no longer walking with God. In fact, I only know two of us who are still here, and we were the only two who got into church. Both he and I have gone through some negative situations with churches. We have both experienced some abusive situations, but we are still here. Even with its problems, the church has many things of value for the believer.

When we first come to a church, we assume that since these people are all Christians they will be easy to relate to. Unfortunately, the opposite is very often true. Sometimes believers are more difficult to relate to than others. The church is full of hurting people who have come to be made whole. Sometimes it takes years for people to work through their problems and until they do, they may be very difficult. Similarly, while we are working through our problems, we may be more difficult than we realize.

In the church, our commitment is to love people while they change. People get saved because they need to change, but it is not our job to produce change. We can give people the tools needed to bring about healthy change, but the choice is theirs. In some cases, we will love them although they may never change. The point is this: it is not our job to decide who should change or when they should change. It is our job to create an environment of love, forgiveness and acceptance that is conducive to change. When and if they change is between them and God. Whether we walk in godly love toward them while they are working out their problems is between us and God. That will be a reflection of the true impact the gospel is having on our lives.

The Apostle John pointed this out in 1 John 4:12, "*If we love one another, God dwelleth in us, and his love is perfected in us.*" God's love is perfected, brought to maturity, accomplishing its goal in us as we love one another. This is a wonderful promise. I can affect the way God's love is developed in my heart by loving others.

The Bible teaches that we reap what we sow. God does not make it happen; it just happens from the laws that He has set in place. If you sow corn, you grow corn. You do not plant corn and grow wheat. The same is true emotionally, physically and spiritually. *"Be not deceived; God is not mocked: for whatsoever a man soweth, that shall he also reap."* Galatians 6:7.

Some principles of sowing and reaping happen through a process called projection. Projection happens when we *project* our values and motives into the actions of others. The Bible calls this judging. When we are kind to others for manipulative, self-centered reasons, we will assume others operate from those same motives. Therefore, when someone is kind to us, we wonder what they really want. We project our motives onto them. We judge them based on our own motives.

We reap exactly what we have sown in our relationships with others. When we sow deceit, we reap mistrust. When we sow manipulation, we reap the fear of being used. When we sow conditional acceptance, we reap rejection. Although another person may be attempting to show us genuine love, we cannot experience it because of the condition of our heart. However, when we begin to love others with no ulterior motives, we become able to receive the love that others attempt to show us. When I love you in your unlovable condition, I can begin to believe that you can love me when I am unlovable.

Walking in love requires the grace of God. God's grace is His power that works in our hearts and makes us able to do the things He requires. It takes the grace of God working in us to love unlovable people. We must seek His grace to walk in love toward undeserving people. We can never do this in our own ability. We must believe and commit ourselves to the grace of God, which makes us able.

The interesting thing about grace is that it is two-sided. The grace that would make us able to give love is the same grace that makes us able to receive love. The Bible presents a clear principle: we cannot receive what we will not give! As I allow God to develop the ability to give freely, I am also allowing Him to develop the ability to receive freely. I only have the capacity to receive from God and people what I have the capacity to give. As I pursue the grace of God to love others, I am also pursuing the grace of God to receive love.

As a part of a local church, I am there to be loved and made whole. I am also there to love others and help them to be made whole. The quality of my relationships is a reflection of the quality of my development in God. It reflects the reality of God's work in my life. It is easy to mysticize my relationship with God. It is easy to deceive myself about my growth and maturity with God. I only *truly* understand what is happening in my growth with God when I look at it alongside my growth in relationships. John says, *"Beloved, let us love one another: for love is of God; and every one that loveth is born of God, and knoweth God. He that loveth not knoweth not God; for God is love."* 1 John 4:7-8.

The mark of knowing and experiencing God is that we love one another. Therefore, walking in love should be our top priority in serving God. All that we would do for God is meaningless if it is not done from the motive of love. There is no spiritual sacrifice, no gift, nothing that replaces walking in love. Paul said in 1 Corinthians 13:1-3, *"Though I speak with the tongues of men and of angels, and have not charity, I am become as sounding brass, or a tinkling cymbal. And though I have the gift of prophecy, and understand all mysteries, and all knowledge; and though I have all faith, so that I could remove mountains, and have not charity, I am nothing. And though I bestow all my goods to feed the poor, and though I give my body to be burned, and have not charity, it profiteth me nothing."*

Apart from love, so-called *spirituality* is meaningless, annoying, profitless, and futile. As a part of a local church, I situationally learn how to relate to God's people. This will be the place where my real spirituality will grow and develop. This will be the place where I will allow the love of God to be perfected in me. This will be where I will see the greatest changes in my life.

This will also be the greatest witnessing tool in my life. The reason the world does not receive the message of the Gospel is that they do not see the proof of its reality. A group of flawless people will not be the proof of our authenticity. It will not be because we have solved all of our problems that the world will want what we have. They will believe we are of God and want what we have when they see us love one another in the face of our flaws. Jesus said it this way, *"By this shall all men know that ye are my disciples, if ye have love one to another."* John 13:35.

There will be nothing more challenging or demanding than a life committed to loving others. It will be in this committed lifestyle that we will grow in the love of God. His love will be perfected in us. It will bring us to the goal that God has for our lives.

Many *loners* withdraw from church and God's people. In that isolation, they falsely assume that they are growing in God. It is easy, when alone, to develop idealistic concepts of life and godliness. When these people try to have involvement with others, however, conflicts and difficulties arise. They mistakenly blame the *unspirituality* of the others as the source of the problems. This becomes justification to withdraw even more.

If God is really working in our lives, we will not need to withdraw to have peace. We will be able to love the unlovable. When we withdraw, we prove that what we have is not genuine and declare that we will not allow God's love to be perfected in us.

Chapter 5

Preserving Purity of Truth

The degree of freedom one experiences will be determined by the degree of truth one knows, believes and puts into practice. Jesus said in John 8:31-32 (The Message Bible), "*If you stick with this, living out what I tell you, you are my disciples for sure. Then you will experience for yourselves the truth, and the truth will free you.*" The integrity of a ministry is greatly revealed by the integrity with which they handle the Word of God. When we depart from the truth, we lead others into destruction. In the Book of Proverbs, God said "*Cease, my son, to hear the instruction that causeth to err from the words of knowledge.*" Proverbs 19:27.

It is every believer's responsibility to determine if they are hearing truth. If what they hear is not truth, they should assume the responsibility to find a church that preaches the truth. We should not continue to expose ourselves to error. Error will always result in destruction.

One of the great responsibilities of the church is to present and preserve truth. The church has the responsibility of teaching the simple truth of God's Word. From the beginning of time, there has been a tendency for people who isolate themselves from meaningful relationships with the fivefold ministry to depart from Bible truth.

One early example of this is a prophet named Balaam. He was a true prophet of God, but he was not involved with Israel. He lived separated from them. In fact, his name literally means "not of the people." Balaam lived apart from God's people. According to the Book of Peter, in that separation he departed from the *right way*. Peter compares those who promise freedom, while dividing churches and sowing discord, to Balaam. Not only are they in error, they have no value for the flock.

If Balaam had not been a loner, it is possible that he would not have gone astray. He still had a gift from God that worked in his life, but he adopted a strange doctrine. He pursued that strange doctrine for personal profit. When we look at the example of Balaam or at the men and women of God who have no personal accountability, or when we look at the people who have isolated themselves and ultimately backslidden, we should take heed.

There is something about involvement with others that keeps us sane and stable. We are not as apt to give ourselves to strange doctrine when we have the accountability of meaningful relationships. We are not as susceptible to sin when we are involved with others. We need others to maintain purity of life and purity of doctrine.

When people have real relationships, it is much more difficult to go astray. Relationships produce genuine accountability. In relationships there are others that can lovingly point it out when we begin to err. Others can help us realize our blind spots and weaknesses.

In every city where Paul started churches, he established oversight. He chose mature, stable men with good reputations and set them in place as leaders. He maintained a relationship with each church through letters, personal visits and through the representatives he sent out to them. One of Paul's major concerns was that people would depart from truth.

In 2 Timothy 4:3-4 Paul warned, *"For the time will come when they will not endure sound doctrine; but after their own lusts shall they heap to themselves teachers, having itching ears; And they shall turn away their ears from the truth, and shall be turned unto fables."* These people who have itching ears (the desire to hear new teaching) depart from sound doctrine. They begin to look to sources outside the church for direction. False teachers in the New Testament present the same problems as false prophets in the Old Testament.

Just as the false prophets led Israel away

from truth, false teachers lead the church away from truth. We live in a day when people are bombarded with teaching, much of which is not based in the New Testament. People are losing their homes, families and all of their life's savings as they listen to teachers who use them for personal gain.

In the Book of Hebrews, Paul gives good guidelines for whom we should follow, *". . . be followers of them who through faith and patience inherit the promises."* Hebrews 6:12. We should know the life of the person we choose to follow. We really do not know if what he preaches is true unless we can observe his life. Several times I have known of people who preached a *spiritual idealism* that was totally unworkable, unscriptural and completely inconsistent with their lives. If I had followed their teaching, I would have ended up with the same problems as them. But as I had the opportunity to observe their lives, I could see that it was not working for them.

One way the church preserves the integrity of the Word is the accountability of relationships. When you can see how a person lives, you know the integrity of their ministry. Similarly, when a person has accountability to the same people regularly, he cannot easily pervert the truth because he is surrounded by those who see his manner of life.

Jesus warned his disciples not to follow

the Pharisees, *"Let them alone: they be blind leaders of the blind. And if the blind lead the blind, both shall fall into the ditch."* Matthew 15:14. He said to leave them alone because if you don't, you will fall into the same ditch they fall into. Today, more than ever, we should heed this admonition. We should not be followers of those who do not have truth working in their lives. We should take heed to whom and what we hear, lest we fall into the ditch.

When we depart from truth, we cut ourselves off from the life and power of God. All that happens in our life with God is a product of believing the truth. When we are separated from truth, in a certain sense, we are separated from God. This does not mean that God has left us, but *we* have left the place where He can work in our lives. It is essential that we continue in the truth.

The Bible is the inspired Word of God. God spoke to us through the Lord Jesus and it was recorded in the scriptures. As problems arose in the early churches, the writers were inspired by the Holy Spirit to answer their questions and solve their difficulties. Those letters (epistles) were passed on to us for our benefit. It is essential that we not depart from the truth of God's Word. To depart from the truth is to depart from God.

The fivefold ministry is a gift to the body of Christ. *"Wherefore he saith, When he ascended up on high, he led captivity captive, and gave gifts unto men . . . And he gave some, apostles; and some, prophets; and some, evangelists; and some, pastors and teachers; For the perfecting of the saints, for the work of the ministry, for the edifying of the body of Christ:"* Ephesians 4:8,11-12. These men and women were specifically commissioned to equip and perfect the saints through the ministry of the Word and through personal involvement.

We are all ministers of the Gospel. We all have a responsibility to preserve and proclaim truth. We all serve to keep one another accountable, yet we must realize that God has specifically entrusted the ministry of the Word to the apostles, prophets, evangelists, pastors and teachers. This does not, by any means, disqualify anyone from ministry. This does not place anyone above another person. It simply points out the different responsibilities we have. It is specifically our job as leaders to equip the saints with the Word of God.

Down through history, there have always been people who sought to undermine and destroy the local church. These are those who, like Balaam, are not of the people. This has been a problem from the beginning. When Paul left Ephesus he warned, *"For I know this, after my departing shall grievous wolves enter in among you, not sparing the flock. Also of your own selves shall men arise, speaking perverse things, to draw away disciples after them."* Acts 20:29-30. Then and now this Word of warning is essential.

There are three primary characteristics in those of whom he warned. First, they have no regard for the *flock.* In other words, they do not see the importance of the local church. They try to break people away from the strength of the congregation. Just as the wolf tries to catch and destroy the stragglers, the wolf Paul warned of tries to catch those who are not close to a local church.

While it is true that there has been much abuse in the body of Christ, this cannot be justification to destroy the one and only organization that Jesus came to establish. The destruction of the church because of its failures would be equivalent to burning the house down because it allows the draft of the winter wind. In the end, instead of being cold, you freeze to death.

The answer to an abusive church is not to reject or seek the destruction of the church; it is simply to find a church that is not abusive. When we separate ourselves from the church, we have separated ourselves from the body. The body needs us and we need the body. The parts cannot survive on their own.

The second characteristic of the wolf is that he speaks perverse things. The word *perverse* means to distort or misinterpret what the Word of God says. Peter 3:16 warns of unlearned and unstable people who twist the scriptures. He points out that their end is always destruction. A common characteristic of all cults is the perversion of the Word of God. So a common way to spot a wolf is the twist he brings to the Word of God. He doesn't deny the Word; he just twists it to his own advantage, or to prove some particular doctrine.

The third characteristic of the wolf, as presented in this passage, is the desire to draw people after themselves. Once they have stripped the believer of his confidence in his church and local leaders, they make themselves to be the answer. "Follow me!" they shout in a voice filled with sincerity and the ring of authenticity. The problem is that they are leading us away from the pattern laid out in the Word of God. They offer us solace from hurt and abuse while they lead us into destruction.

James 1:20 says this, "*The wrath of man worketh not the righteousness of God.*" Creating anger toward anyone or anything is not the way to solve our problems. The Bible clearly teaches that anger gives place to the devil. While creating anger against the church, they also create a blindness that keeps us from seeing the trap that lies ahead. We should vehemently resist those who would isolate us from others, especially by creating anger and offense.

While the church has had many faults and at times has been the source of error, it is still God's plan. To draw away from error is essential, but to isolate ourselves from others will usually end with our becoming as corrupt as that which we despise. With all its flaws, the church has preserved the basic body of truth for nearly two thousand years. It has been those who have isolated themselves that have abandoned basic, Bible truth.

If you do not believe what your church preaches, the answer is not isolation. The answer is to find those of "like-faith." If those of like-faith do not live in victory, do not maintain good relationships, or there is not good fruit, then maybe you need to reexamine your beliefs.

Chapter 6

A Place of Growth and Service

In Ephesians 4 it gives the goal of both the fivefold ministry and those who receive that ministry. It is the goal of the ministry to perfect, make whole, mend and equip the saints. That equipping should bring each person to the place of ministry to others. Frankly, all real growth brings us a step closer to a servant's heart.

In Ephesians 2:10 it says, *"For we are his workmanship, created in Christ Jesus unto good works, which God hath before ordained that we should walk in them."* While we are set free from works for righteousness sake, we are created unto good works. With God's nature in us, we cannot help but do the same things God does. The Bible says, *". . . as He is, so are we in this world."* 1 John 4:17.

Because we were created in the likeness and image of God, we have a need to be life givers. There is something in our new nature that needs to be involved with giving the love and life of God to people. We are called to bear fruit. We are created in a way that demands we live for a cause outside of ourselves. The ministry of the local church equips and facilitates that cause. We are in the process of being equipped to do the work of the ministry.

Not only is the church a place of preparation for service, it is also a place for finding and directing our gifts and creative skills. It is in a local body of believers that we find many of our opportunities of service. Most people will not discover ministry on their own; therefore, they will have a great void in their life. But those who are a part of a local body usually find opportunities to utilize their ministry gifts.

One of the greatest misconceptions of the dark ages was that ministry belonged to the clergy. The truth is, most meaningful ministry belongs to the church member. You are the body, you are the one who is in touch with the real needs of society. You will contact people that the average minister will never meet. You will be the one who evangelizes your neighborhood and work place. You will be the one who has the first opportunity to minister to the other members of the body.

Most people will never discover and develop their areas of personal ministry without help and direction. Through involvement with a local church, the needs of the body and the needs of the community can be discovered. Through Biblical teaching we can be prepared for the work of the ministry. Through the example of mature believers we can be inspired to serve the needs of humankind.

According to a study done by Stanford University, 95% of what a person learns in a seminar is of no value. This is because they do not know how to put it into practice. I believe these same figures could apply to the average church member. Most of what they hear in church never helps them. The problem is seldom that they are not hearing the truth; the problem is they do not know how to put that truth into practice in a real life setting.

It therefore, becomes the job of the local church to facilitate the application of truth. One of the greatest ways this will happen will be as we serve one another in love—as we step outside of our selfish existence and PUT TRUTH INTO PRACTICE!

We do not *really* know anything that we have not put into practice. Until we can use it in a real life setting, it is only theory to us. Unfortunately, if we wait until we are in trouble to trust God in an area, we will lack the confidence to follow Him. But when we minister to others, we see truth work. We learn about the practical side of truth. Then because we have had personal experience, we are prepared to apply truth in our own life without fear.

Jesus trained His disciples in an uncommon way. He did not remove them from ministry to teach them the truth. He kept them in the middle of life's realities. He did not load them down with truth for three years and then send them out to figure out how to put it into practice. He never taught them in theory beyond what they could put into practice. He would not allow their exposure to truth to exceed their experience.

Jesus never taught His disciples *how* to minister. He taught them the same truth He taught everyone else. He taught them about life, about a relationship with God, about personal things, and as they ministered to others they saw the reality of those truths. He did not teach them how to cast out devils; He taught them that they had power over demons, demonstrated it in their presence and then gave them the opportunity to do the same. He never taught them how to get healed; He taught them the truth about healing, and then ministered healing to the sick. From this they learned not only how to minister healing to others, but also how to walk in healing for themselves. He always gave them the chance to *put it into practice.*

Years later, the Apostle Paul was writing to the church at Philippi and said, *"Whatever you have learned or received or heard from me, or seen in me - put into practice. And the God of peace will be with you."* Philippians 4:9 NIV. They were not going to experience the God of peace simply by believing something; they had to believe and put it into practice.

The church provides us with a way to put what we have learned into practice. It facilitates serving God and serving God's people. It will be the launching pad into our personal ministry. The church will also be the proving ground for the truth we receive.

Whatever our special talent may be, there is going to be a place in the church to use that for God and His people. There are those who need for you to fulfill your God-given destiny. The entire body lacks until each person does their part. Without each member functioning the church will never be what it should be. The following quotation says it best; *"It was He who gave some to be apostles, some to be prophets, some to be evangelists, and some to be pastors and teachers, to prepare God's people for works of service, so that the body of Christ may be built up, . . . as each member does its work."* Ephesians 4:11-12,16 NIV.

Discover, commit to, and prepare to serve God. When you become a part of a local church get involved with the areas of ministry where you have an interest. If they do not have anything in your area of interest, start something. Do not allow the body to lack because you do not do your part.

The day you put your name on a church roll, should be the day that you make a commitment to some area of serving in that church. As a part of the family, you should assume your responsibility.

In deciding where you attend church, this should be a factor. Will they allow me to serve? Will they train me to serve? Do not become a part of a church that will not help develop you for service.

A major part of being emotionally attached to a church occurs through your area of serving. Unless one assumes his personal responsibilities, he will never feel like a part of things. There will always be something lacking in a relationship where one receives, but never gives.

Finding your place of serving meets a need in you. It meets a need in those you serve. It gives you an emotional tie and becomes an essential part of your personal growth.

Chapter 7

The Power of the Group

Besides all of the previously mentioned reasons for participating in a local church, the Bible tells us *"And let us consider one another to provoke unto love and to good works: Not forsaking the assembling of ourselves together, as the manner of some is."* Hebrews 10:24-25. God commands us to assemble together. The benefits of assembling together are far too numerous to list in detail, but I think there are a few we should discuss.

The church is described as a body: the body of Christ. One of the unique aspects of the body is *synergy*. Synergy is the combined actions of the organs of the body. The body works through synergy. It is not what one organ can do that is as important as what organs working together can do. For example, the heart is responsible for pumping the blood through the vessels. But the heart could never do this alone. Without all of the other organs functioning properly, the heart would not pump the blood through the body. Every part depends on other parts to do its work.

Synergy is important in the use of drugs,

vitamins and herbs when used for healing purposes. There are things that accomplish more by the combined effects of one or more elements than by the individual effects of any single element. In a certain sense, when two elements are used together they become something different. They can accomplish something that neither of them could accomplish on their own.

This is why the Bible describes a man and woman marrying and becoming one flesh. Two parts of the body of Christ come together and become something they were not before. As a team, they can accomplish things that could never be done individually. Similarly, when we are in Christ, we become new creatures. By joining ourselves to Him, we become something new and different, something we could never become on our own. It is the same with a local church. Together, the members of that body become something that they could never be on their own. This applies to many aspects of Christian life.

The unique thing about the synergy created by becoming a part of the body is that we never lose our individuality. We never melt into the oblivion of a group. We retain our identity, individuality and uniqueness: the wonderful aspects of our intimate life in God that can never be a part of the public experience. God relates to us as individuals, but together we become and experience things that are impossible as an individual.

In a group we have the opportunity to experience and express praise and worship. There are many different aspects to praise and worship. There should be private praise and worship, but private does not replace public or vice versa.

When people are first saved or first baptized in the Holy Spirit, they have no real idea about how to praise and worship. It is one of those things we see in the Bible, yet have no real concept of how it is done. In corporate worship, we enter in with the group. We gain freedom from the freedom of the group. We become inspired to express our intimate feelings for God as we see others' example.

In this setting, people often open themselves up to the gifts of the Spirit for the first time. We see others move in their spiritual gifts and we gain understanding about what is happening in us.

I had been moving in prophesy for over a year before I really knew what it was. When I saw someone being used to *bring a word* for the first time, I understood what was happening in me. I learned many things about laying on of hands, casting out demons and other areas of ministry as I observed them in a public worship service. I grew in my confidence in every area of praise and worship as I participated with the group. Today, my greatest fulfillment in praise and worship is not with the group, it is when I am alone with God. Yet I realize that the group still needs me and I still need the group. I need to be there leading the way just as others were there for me. I need the group when my heart is hard or when I am having difficulty responding to God.

When I was first saved, I really did not feel that I needed people. I had learned to survive on my own. I was willing to serve others because it was pleasing to God, but the truth was I did not think I needed anyone. As I have grown in God, I have daily realized how deep my need is for Him. Similarly, as I have grown in God I have continually grown in my realization of my need for His people. I need the church!

When becoming a part of the church, most people are either independent or co-dependent. We rarely change from that initial frame of mind. The independent ones, like me, do not need anyone. We are there doing our own thing, pitying those poor, weak people who need others. Then there are the co-dependent ones: those who come in and have a very unhealthy need of others. They go to the other extreme. They do not feel they can exist without others.

Both types of people are equally disturbed. They are both bound for a fall. The co-dependent will fall because of disappointment. Co-dependent people have expectations of others. They need for others to be a certain way in order to meet their needs. When others fail to live up to those expectations, the co-dependent person feels wronged and offended. Then they reject others for not living up to their expectations. The independent person may be judgmental of those who have needs. They expect everyone to live up to their personal standards. The independent person despises the weak and does not see that he would ever need any of these people. In that judgmental arrogance, he drifts away.

What both of these people need is the realization that we can live without one another, but there are certain needs that can only be met through our involvement with others. Some people describe this as interdependence. In interdependence, we choose to open ourselves up to others. We choose to allow others to have healthy relationships with us.

Because of the way we were created, we gain a sense of identity from the group with which we are involved. Because we are social beings, we need to identify with others. We look for others who will accept us. To a certain degree, we determine who we are by the group that accepts us.

My identity should come from my personal relationship with God more than any other place. I should see whom He has made me to be in Jesus, and I should accept that reality. That will never happen if I am isolated from the group that identifies with God.

Because I am a social being, I will be involved with some group. Some people go to a bar and talk to nearly no one, yet they are a part of that group: the barroom group. That is how they see themselves. There are even people who isolate themselves at home and never go out, yet through television or radio they find someone with whom they can identify. Though it is an illusion, they identify with groups of people on television. One way or another, imaginary or real, we will find a group with which to identify.

Once we have found the group we identify with, we will begin to modify our behavior, our characteristics, our way of dressing and the way we talk to be more like the group. In other words, we will take on the image of the group. This now becomes the way we see ourselves, our self-image.

Eventually, we will derive our worth from the value the group has for us. Self-worth is never found in personal achievements. It is only how those achievements make us appear to the group that gives it meaning. We were created to derive worth from a source outside of ourselves. Ultimately, that source should be God and His great value for us, but the value that God has for us is closely associated with the value God's people have for us. Without a sense of value from God's people, we will look in other places for acceptance and worth. When we find that other place, we will conform to what will give us acceptance with that group. In short, we backslide!

When people cannot find a way to have a meaningful relationship with God's people, they have a sense of emptiness. They have needs that are not being met. Becoming a real part of the group does mean change. Since we so deeply fear change, we stay on the outside of the group. We are never a part. We do not find our place. It is just a matter of time before we backslide. It is not a question of *if* we will backslide, it is only a matter of *when*.

We have a need to be accepted by a group. If we do not feel that we can make the changes necessary to have a relationship, or if we are unwilling, we will look for a source that does not require as much from us. But we will eventually find a place of acceptance.

In the Bible, God gives more than 360 instructions to leaders about ministry to and involvement with the congregation. There has never been a time when God presented a concept of man surviving on his own. While we are all priests and kings under the new covenant, man still has the same basic needs for others. For that reason, Jesus clearly presented the reality of establishing the church as His body.

Chapter 8

Challenged to Grow

We are challenged to grow through involvement with people. This is why some people dread involvement. As we become involved and interdependent, we are forced to change. This is what the Bible means when it says, "*Iron sharpeneth iron; so a man sharpeneth the countenance of his friend.*" Proverbs 27:17.

An individual who does not have the confidence to change is limited in his scope of friendship. He is limited in his growth in God. This individual will be threatened by every aspect of relationships. The challenges of growth will become a threat and he will draw back from involvement.

There is no growth apart from challenges. The condition of our heart determines if we see something as a challenge or a threat. Many people view the Word of God as a threat. It threatens their security; therefore, they are easily offended. We must realize that the Word that has the greatest potential to set us free also has the greatest potential to offend us.

Every problem I have is the result of the things I believe and do. For my life to change, I must do things differently than I have ever done them. Therefore, I must believe something differently than I previously believed. All it takes for me to have the same problems next year that I had last year is to keep doing and believing the same things.

I do things the way I do because I think that is the right way. "*There is a way that seemeth right unto a man, but the end thereof are the ways of death.*" Proverbs 16:25. What I think is the right way may really be what is causing all of the pain in my life. However, I cannot see that because I think I'm doing it the right way. I think something else must be causing this pain.

The moment I do find the right way, I am brought face to face with the fact that I have been doing or believing something wrong. If my self-worth is wrapped up in being right, I will be offended. Therefore, the truth that was intended to set me free, offended me. I will not only be offended at the truth, I will be offended at the person who brings that truth. Thus, out of my need to be right, I destroy my relationship with the group and begin to seek out a new place of acceptance.

One can always find people who will accept his opinions (beliefs). We may find them in jail, in the hospital, or in a cult. We may find them with a group of backslidden, out of church, offended people. But be assured, we can find them. When we do, we will reinforce our already wrong beliefs and actions and we will assure that our life will stay the same.

"*All scripture is given by inspiration of God, and is profitable for doctrine, for reproof, for correction, for instruction in righteousness: That the man of God may be perfect, thoroughly furnished unto all good works.*" 2 Timothy 3:16-17. All scripture is true and will ultimately bring freedom, peace and joy. But scripture is not only used to edify and build up; it is also used to correct, reprove and instruct.

The Bible says that chastisement is never joyful. The word *chastise* does not mean to whip. It is not a negative word, it means to child-train. Unfortunately, much of child-training is correction. When people are headed in a destructive direction, they need to hear the truth. If their heart is not open and teachable, it will be an unpleasant experience. If they are open and teachable, it will be a joy to discover the truth. "*Give instruction to a wise man, and he will be yet wiser: teach a just man, and he will increase in learning.*" Proverbs 9:9.

A fool despises correction and instruction. He sees it as a threat to his self-worth. To the fool, being right is more important than discovering what is right. "*The way of a fool is right in his own eyes: but he that hearkeneth unto counsel is wise.*" Proverbs 12:15.

It is never the job of leaders to run another person's life. People should be allowed to make their own decisions. It is not the place of the church to violate the will of anyone. Each person must stand or fall by his own decisions. But it *is* the place of the minister to present truth from the pulpit and in counsel. After leaders have lovingly presented the truth, it is then the choice of the person to accept that truth.

When a person deems that something is true, it is then his responsibility to take that truth before God and find the wisdom to implement it in his own life. There, in your prayer closet, you find the application of that truth.

There is always a time, in this process of discovering truth, when we have the opportunity to be offended. It is in that moment, when our heart is being challenged by the Word of God, when we choose life or death, blessings or curses. This is the time that we really discover our submission to the Lordship of Jesus.

This does not mean that every word that a minister shares with us is what we need. It is our job, however, to take counsel before the Lord to consider its validity. Every word of advice must be weighed in the scripture. There will be times when it is appropriate to kindly do something that is different from the counsel we receive.

Every person will stand before God for himself. Your pastor, mother, father, husband or wife will not be with you. You will give an account of what you have done in this life.

Therefore, the ultimate responsibility for deciding what you should do falls on your own shoulders. You must look to the Word of God for yourself. You must pray for yourself. You must take the information given to you and you must make the final decision for your life. You are the one who must live with the results.

Through the teaching of the Word, through personal counsel, through the gifts of the Holy Spirit and through personal relationships we are challenged to grow and change. That does not mean that we will not be loved or accepted if we do not change. It simply means that being a part of a group always challenges us to grow.

We must never give up our individuality in the name of growth. We do not need to change our personality. We simply learn to walk in our strengths rather than our weaknesses. It is essential that we never confuse growth and conformity. Growth is a development of character where our motives are refined. We begin to operate in love. We look to the good of others. We leave selfish and self-centered behavior behind.

Conformity is where we change our personality. We conform externally for the acceptance of the group. Conformity is totally destructive. It is the ultimate of rejection. It demands that we surrender who we are to be accepted. Conformity will produce self-deceit, and will eventually produce wrath and anger.

God needs you. He does not need your impersonation of someone else. But He does need for you to have character and integrity. Involvement with a group does mean that we must walk in integrity. It does mean we must temper our behavior by our character for the good of all.

One of the greatest temptations to withdraw from the body of Christ comes out of an insecurity that resists change. No matter how destructive, we all want to justify our way of doing things. We need to be right to establish a false sense of self-worth. In so doing, we find a comfort zone where we are never challenged to grow.

Chapter 9

Relating to Oversight

Because of abuses, both leaders and followers have overreacted to one another. This overreaction has caused the development of strange doctrine from the leaders and bad attitudes from the people.

Leaders have overreacted to the lack of commitment of the people. From that, they have developed doctrines of control and domination. People have overreacted to the control of leaders and have developed attitudes of rebellion and defiance. Both extremes are deadly for the individuals, for the church and for the world.

Leaders are afraid to give people freedom. Because of the already deficient commitment that exists among members, the leader fears that any more freedom will produce the destruction of the individual and the church. Members are afraid of commitment. They are afraid they will be abused. Too often they have seen the committed being used and abused.

The abuses that exist in churches do not justify bad attitudes and lack of commitment on our part. After all, our real commitment is to Jesus. We do what we do for the good of the people and we do it unto the Lord. When the church begins to draw us into a commitment that is unhealthy, it is our place to do something about it. We have the option of saying "No" when we need to. Failure to exercise that option is a personal failure. If we do not say "No," we cannot claim abuse. We can only look to our own heart to find the problem.

To understand commitment, it may be necessary to understand abuse. Abuse is a participatory experience. It is never the product of one person. It takes cooperation for us to be abused. We have, to a certain degree, created the situation in which we are abused. Just yesterday, I met with a family who had all been in an abusive church situation. As I shared the truth with them, it was a time of real soul searching.

I gently looked them in the eye and said, "You were getting something out of that situation, or you would not have allowed it." That seems like a hard thing to say to someone who has been hurt, but it is a truth we must face. We must ask ourselves   "What need was I getting met by staying in an abusive situation?"

As each of the family members thought about this question, they each reached their own conclusion. One by one each of them realized totally different needs that were being met by cooperating with that abusive situation. They realized they were participating in their own destruction. They realized that they were using the leader as much as the leader was using them.

They were trying to get a need met; they had participated in their own abuse.

After spending a year out of the ministry because of hurt and anger at the church, God began drawing me back. I fearfully resisted. I did not want to be abused by the people. I feared being back in that position where people looked to me and blamed me for things in their own life.

As the Lord was speaking to me one day He said, "You try to do for people what I will not even do for them." I found that quite shocking, but as I looked back over my ministerial history, I saw that I had a view of ministry that was not scriptural. I saw that the accepted paradigm for ministry was very destructive. I saw that we spent our entire time dealing with issues that could only be settled between that person and Jesus.

Similarly, I see that people draw leaders into their problems. There is a real affinity toward involving leaders in situations where they should never be involved. Much abuse happens because we invite others into private areas of our lives. Usually, we draw others into our situations because we want them to declare us *right*. We do not really want the truth; we simply want them to agree with *our* version of the truth.

Once, while Jesus was preaching, a man came to Him to present a personal problem. *"And one of the company said unto him, Master, speak to my brother, that he divide the inheritance with me."* Luke 12:13. I have no idea what the man's motive was. He could have been genuine in his desires or he may simply have wanted Jesus to take his side. Regardless, Jesus' reply was surprising. *"And he said unto him, Man, who made me a judge or a divider over you?"* Luke 12:14. Jesus refused to be drawn into situations that overstepped the bounds of individual choice.

Any good pastor would have been drawn into that situation, but Jesus was not. This was an area that had to be resolved by their own integrity. More than once, I have been drawn into a person's life in areas where I should not have been. I thought what I was doing was the work of a good minister, but I have since learned that I cannot allow people to draw me into certain areas of their life. In the end, if those situations do not work out the way the person wants, I get the blame. If that person does not trust my advice, in the end, they will accuse me of misleading them.

As leaders, we should give scriptural advice. But it is the responsibility of that person to find how that advice will work in their particular situation. It is also their responsibility to get the grace of God to apply truth. We cannot make decisions for others and we cannot do for others what they will not do for themselves.

I once had a woman come to me about some problems in her marriage. Her husband was very dominating and demanding. He had total control of her and the children. She wanted me to confront the husband. In the past, this same situation had occurred. She had gone to leaders and gotten them involved. In the end, when she did not have the courage to follow through, the husband ultimately caused her to back down. He then became angry at the church for getting involved in his private life. From his perspective, the church was trying to influence his wife against him.

This woman was a very kind and sweet individual. She really needed some relief. Her situation was quite difficult, but I was unable to help her. I suggested some things that she should do. I assured her that if she would implement this truth for ninety days, I would then be willing to talk to the husband. But if she could not apply the truth for ninety days, then she would be unable to withstand him even if I talked to him and caused a change. She needed to trust God for grace in her situation.

She was unable to walk this out. She could not get the courage to apply the truth we had agreed upon, therefore, I knew I could not help her. It would have been very easy for me to start making decisions for her. I could have easily justified my involvement by the difficulty of her situation. It would have been very easy for me to cross the line in my responsibilities and her's. In the end, I would have been trying to work out her salvation instead of leaving that for her. It would have become an abusive situation. She was asking me to do for her what she would not do for herself. If I created her freedom, I would have to maintain her freedom. Actually, she would not have been free; she would have only been controlled by someone other than her husband—her pastor.

Any way we look at it, abuse is two-way participation. Whether we are leaders or church members, we must accept our responsibility for being involved in an abusive situation. Neither side must blame the other. We must both accept that we are getting some kind of need met in our lives, or we would not cross the line. For the church member, it is usually a matter of acceptance. For the leader, it is usually a matter of feeling needed.

It is the duty of leaders to lead. Leaders are people of purpose and passion. They are on their way and others follow them in pursuit of their dreams. Jesus established leadership. He said they were gifts to the body. Their gift keeps us on track. Their passion motivates them to seek God and bring inspiration and direction to the body. We cannot simply reject leadership because we have had a bad experience along the way.

Hebrews 13:17 reads as follows, *"Obey*

*them that have the rule over you, and submit
yourselves: for they watch for your souls, as they
that must give account, that they may do it with
joy, and not with grief: for that is unprofitable
for you.*" A close look at this scripture in the
original language reveals something quite
different. No leader actually *rules over* anyone.
Leaders are simply servants. It is the job of the
leader to serve others as they walk with God.

For more detail of this verse, you may
refer to my book entitled, "<u>Leadership That
Builds People.</u>" This verse is more appropriately
translated as, *"Yield to, win the favor of those
who go before you and submit yourselves, for they
watch for your souls as they that must minister the
word, that they may do it with joy and not with
grief; for that is unprofitable for you."*
We should follow leaders in a way that is
pleasant for them and us. Hebrews 6:12 does say
that we should follow those who, through faith
and patience, inherit the promises. In other
words, if they do not have truth working in their
lives, we should not follow them. A person's
position does not give him dominion over
another. A person's position does not mean that
we should blindly follow their advice. How well
an individual preaches is not proof of his insight.
The level of the truth working in his life is the
determining factor about whom we should follow.
Only a fool follows a fool. Neither should we

look at the mystical areas of his life. Instead, we need to look at practical areas: Does he walk in love? Does he have a good family life? Does he walk in integrity and morality? Does he receive the promises of God? If not, he may be a kind man; but we can lovingly decline to follow his leadership.

It is not the job of the leader to decide what we should do with our lives. It is the job of the leader to help us accomplish what we desire to accomplish with our lives. The leader serves us by giving us truth and a godly example of how to live a victorious life. Similarly, we as members of the body, serve to help one another become victorious in life. If any person stops serving others and looks only to be served, destruction is on the way.

A leader cannot insist that people serve the church when he is not serving the people. The people cannot insist that the leaders serve them and not be willing to serve others. We are all servants. We all bring our talents, gifts and strengths to the church for the common good of all. Every person should seek to do his part.

Paul describes this best when ministering to the church at Ephesus. These were among the last words he ever spoke to them, *"I have showed you all things, how that so labouring ye ought to support the weak, and to remember the words of the Lord Jesus, how he said, It is more blessed to give than to receive."* Acts 20:35. Paul presents the real fruit of Christianity: to love and serve one another.

Jesus, Himself, set the example that we should not look to be served, but to serve others. *"For even the Son of man came not to be ministered unto, but to minister, and to give his life a ransom for many."* Mark 10:45. As we follow Him, we emulate servanthood. It is impossible to follow Him and not be a servant. *"And he said to them all, If any man will come after me, let him deny himself, and take up his cross daily, and follow me. For whosoever will save his life shall lose it: but whosoever will lose his life for my sake, the same shall save it."* Luke 9:23-24.

Just as abuse is a two-way relationship, so is serving. We should go into a church expecting to have certain needs met, but we should also go into a church looking to meet certain needs. One should never become part of a local church without making a commitment to serve the people of that church. It is not abuse or control when leaders expect us to serve. Just as we have the right to expect things from leaders, leaders have the right to expect things from us. What we should *all* expect is to serve one another in love.

If every member does their part, there will be no lack in the body. No one must give too much or work too much if every member does their part. It is when members fail to assume their responsibility to serve that leaders fall prey to the pressures. Those pressures are then passed along to the congregation. The congregation resents the pressure and draws back. The leader resents the apathy and presses harder. Thus, the syndrome is in full bloom.

It does not matter what another person's motives may be, I must serve God and His people out of the purity of my own heart. I must do what I do *unto the Lord.* I must never serve for the approval of the leader. I must say "No" to areas of responsibility that are beyond my ability or desire.

I must recognize that the leaders will have direction and strategies. I must realize that becoming part of any church is saying, to some degree, that I can acceptably serve God while moving in the direction of this local church. I want to fulfill my vision, but I also want to be a part of helping others fulfill their vision. Being part of a local church is like being part of any family, you make sacrifices for the group and the group sacrifices for you.

Just as an abusive relationship is participatory, a healthy relationship is much more so. I must make every effort to *know those that labor among us.* I should assume the responsibility to have a favorable relationship. I must allow the leader to speak into my life, but all of this should be done out of a commitment to the Lord. It must never be a means of earning favor, approval or acceptance.

God has called us to commitment, not co-dependency. I must have a healthy relationship with leadership. I must never look to them to do for me what only Jesus can do. I must not have unrealistic expectations of any leader. A leader cannot be a substitute for knowing God. His words cannot replace the Word of God. His acceptance can never replace the acceptance of God. He is not a substitute for my natural father. He is my friend and co-laborer in Christ. He has a specific role in my life. I should honor and respect him as much as possible, but I should also realize he should never have more influence in my life than Jesus.

The leader will have a God-given plan for this church. I must have a God-given plan for my life. It is up to me to determine if the plan for my life can fit into the plan for the church.

Chapter 10

The Church has Changed

In my early days as a minister, as I examined the early church in the Book of Acts, my idealism said, "Let's get rid of buildings, they didn't have buildings. Let's get rid of structure; they didn't have structure. Let's get rid of everything that I can't see in the Book of Acts." I thought I was committed to doing things the Bible way, but I soon learned I was just ignorant and idealistic. My idealism was blinding me to obvious realities that I was incapable of understanding.

The early church was actually very structured. We just do not have much written material about its structure. Why? The method of structure is not that important. There are many different ways to administrate. The method is not good or bad in itself; it is the motive and the wisdom that validates the method. The method is completely adjustable to the needs.

The New Testament is unclear about many things. When it is unclear, I have come to understand that it is not essential. Unfortunately, we have focused on the nonessentials to the demise of the essentials. We have more conflict about methodology than about truth. We should commit ourselves to the truth, but we should remain flexible about methodology.

In my immaturity, I thought it was the emergence of buildings and structure that destroyed the spiritual life of the early church. Now, I understand that it is the hearts of men that determine if there is life or death in the church. Buildings, structure, church government and many other things are means of serving the people. These things are the tools that make it possible to minister to a variety of people. There is no right or wrong church government. Having or not having a building, how many deacons you have, or your definition of elders is all immaterial until you look at the motive behind it. All these things can be exceedingly good or exceedingly evil. What determines their validity is whether they are used to control the people or serve the people.

As the early church grew, its needs changed. They prayerfully adapted to those emerging needs. For example, there was nothing holy about having seven deacons. They simply felt seven deacons could meet the needs that were present at that time. When they appointed seven deacons, they had thousands of members. I can remember being in very small churches that thought they should have seven deacons, because the church in Acts had seven. By the time you take seven deacons out of a church of 60 people, you've taken all the people who want to serve. Your church may not need seven deacons; it may only need one or two, or even none.

There are many titles and structures that we fight about. The truth is, there is room in every church for whatever kinds of positions are needed to minister to the needs of the people. There is room for different kinds of church government. Every church should decide what is best for itself. Find what works. Find what brings fruitfulness and peace. Throw away your religious paradigms. They only cause arguments, divisions, and strife.

As the needs of the church have evolved, the church has failed to be flexible and adaptable to meet those needs. We have strived to salvage and sustain our ideas more than to meet the needs of the people. Truth is absolute; however, the application of truth is completely variable. We must never depart from scriptural principle, but we should continually renew our antiquated views of application.

The church has been very slow to realize and meet the needs of its people. Most of our current evangelism is a feeble attempt to win back the children that the last generation lost. We have failed to maintain ground. We have failed to present the gospel in a way that is attractive, desirable, and effective. Proverbs 25:11 says, "*A word fitly spoken is like apples of gold in settings of silver."* A word *fitly spoken* is a word that is presented in an attractive way. Titus 2:10 in the NIV says, ". . . *in every way . . . make the teaching about God our Savior attractive."*

Because we have not been responsive to the needs of society, we have failed to make the gospel attractive. We have stayed twenty or more years behind current thought and current needs. We are out of touch with the thoughts, needs, and trends of the society we are trying to reach. We have made it quite unattractive and difficult to become a Christian.

Buildings, attractive grounds, innovative music, creative and exciting children's ministry are all parts of presenting the gospel (apples of gold) in an attractive format (settings of silver). These things are not the goals of the gospel or the proof of God's blessing, nor are they the earmarks of our personal success. They should not be the things we strive for. They should simply be tools that we use to be more effective at ministering to the people we currently have, and reaching the people we do not have.

If we want our children to grow up and know God, we must compete with *MTV, The Power Rangers* and every conceivable cartoon show. We must present the truth in a way that holds their interest and stimulates their hunger and curiosity. We must have a children's ministry that is innovative and exciting.

If we are to meet the needs that exist in society, we must have good counseling programs. We need counselors that understand the complex needs of substance abusers, sexual abuse, co-dependency and all the other great needs of society.

We must have a more diverse ministry team than ever imagined. We must have youth and teen leaders that can relate to today's youth. They must be people who understand the pressures of that group. They must be people who speak the language and understand the needs. We must step out of the dark ages. What worked last year may not work this year—even though the truth is the same. Only the truth will help people, but people will never hear truth if we cannot present it in a way that is acceptable to the society we are trying to reach.

The heading to Psalm 84 in the Amplified Bible reads, *"To the Chief Musician; set to a Philistine lute, or (possibly) a particular Gittite tune."* In other words, the Psalmist took an inspired Psalm of God and put it to contemporary music. Truth is holy, but there is nothing holy or unholy about methodology and style. We must use every available tool if we are to reach and keep the people of our society. Jesus said we were to be fishers of men—good fishermen always use the best bait.

We have not been left in this world for the mere pleasure of existence. We will have an eternity of pleasurable existence. We are here to serve God and man by reaching our world with the gospel of the Lord Jesus Christ. Then we are to make disciples of those we reach, so they can live a victorious life and reach others. To fulfill this, we must commit ourselves completely to the truth, the task and the methodology that work.

The only similarity between today's church and the early church is the truth we embrace. The methodology should be as diverse as the culture we try to reach. The style of music we play, the way we dress in church, even our style of preaching should be determined by what is effective. When Paul went to the Gentiles he changed his name and cut his beard. He did what was completely unacceptable to his religious culture, but it was totally acceptable and effective for reaching the Greeks. When Paul had Timothy circumcised, it had nothing to do with his Old Covenant beliefs, it was for effectiveness with the Jews. Paul said, *"For though I be free from all men, yet have I made myself servant unto all, that I might gain the more. And unto the Jews I became as a Jew, that I might gain the Jews; to them that are under the law, as under the law, that I might gain them that are under the law; To them that are without law, as without law, (being not without law to God, but under the law to*

Christ,) that I might gain them that are without law. To the weak became I as weak, that I might gain the weak: I am made all things to all men, that I might by all means save some. And this I do for the gospel's sake, that I might be partaker thereof with you." 1 Corinthians 9:19-23.

Your paradigm of church may be the thing that makes you unhappy with your church. You go into a church expecting it to be like it was when you were a child, like a church in another city, or you want your city church to be like the rural church. Your expectancy can cause you great trepidation or dissatisfaction, but even worse, it can cause great ineffectiveness.

Before you decide what kind of church you want, ask yourself "Will the kind of church I want meet the needs of the people? Can it reach our community?" In certain communities it is essential to have a large attractive building, otherwise the people of that community will not respond to you. In other areas, a plush church would turn people away.

In a rural church the music needs a country flavor. In a young community the music needs to be more contemporary. In some settings, only traditional church music will be accepted. It is not a question of right or wrong; it is a question of what is effective.

The truth is absolute and will never change, but the truth will always cross cultural, social and international boundaries. The church is a living organism, it has changed and will keep on changing in order to effectively facilitate truth.

We all pray for revival, but resist change. We only need revival if what we previously had, failed. If what we had failed, then we do not need it again. We need something different.

The reason churches get left behind is they refuse to change and adapt to what is effective for this time, culture and present needs. Hold fast to the truth, but allow God to cause the change that will make truth effective in your life.

Chapter 11

Your Church
My Ministry

Among the many paradoxes that we have failed to grasp, this one has caused as many disappointed expectations as any. "Whose church is it, anyway?" is a legitimate question of the church member. "I've got to do the will of God!" is the emphatic stand of the minister. It seems these two positions can never meet on friendly ground. Both parties feel they will somehow "lose" if they allow the other to get what they want.

In our linear, "either/or" thinking, we have not understood that these are separate issues. Because of the battle over the church and ministry, we put the minister and the member in a win or lose, succeed or fail position. We cannot see that both parties should win in this battle. The minister can have his ministry and fulfill his call; the church members can have the church they want. Neither party must become subject to the control of the other.

Without a doubt, the minister must fulfill his call as he sees fit. This does not mean he is unaccountable. It does not mean that he fails to receive meaningful direction or counsel. Only a fool fails to listen to those whom he is serving. That is, of course, if serving is the minister's goal. We cannot effectively serve our people if we do not listen to them. That is like the retailer who does not know what the people want to buy. He may have good products, a beautiful store and wonderful clerks, but if he does not have what the people need and want, he will not last in business. He may have the warmest, fleece-lined coats at the best price in the entire world, but they won't sell on Miami Beach when people want to buy bathing suits.

It has been my observation that churches and businesses fail at about the same rate. Because we have spiritualized the failure of churches, we have not learned much from those failures. It is my belief that churches and businesses fail for the same reasons: they do not meet the needs of the people. Until we hear the cry of the people, we will not understand why churches fail. There is no room for idealism and over-opinionation in serving people. We must hear the voice of the people we serve.

Every minister should minister in a way that he believes is acceptable to God. He will stand alone before God and give an account of his life and ministry. He must, therefore, have a sense of following the direction of the Lord. He must minister in a way that is consistent with his own beliefs. Yet he must still listen to the people. It is, after all, the people that the minister is seeking to serve.

The ministers in the early church listened to the complaints of the people in Acts when the Grecian widows were being overlooked in the administration of daily needs. The office of the deacon was not established because the Holy Spirit first led them to do it. Quite the contrary, when the leaders realized there was a need, they sought God for a plan that would work to meet the need. The church in Acts would have had a major split had they not responded to the needs of the people. God is always ready to give us a plan that meets the needs of the people. It is not rebellion or an attack on leadership when people declare their needs. It is the information we need in order to be effective minsters.

While people often misunderstand what will help them, they usually know their own needs. We cannot always minister to people the way they want, but we can meet the needs they present to us. Therefore, we must listen to them. We must hear what their needs are, and then we, as leaders, must find a scripturally consistent way to help them.

The minister sets the tone and establishes the "flavor" of the ministry. His methodology is revealed in the way he ministers individually and from the pulpit. There are as many different acceptable methods of ministry as there are different kinds of people. The minister must evaluate the effectiveness of how he ministers. He must decide if his type of ministry is meaningful to the people he is serving. He must continually adjust what he is doing to meet the needs of the people.

Just as the minister sets the tone of the ministry, the members determine the "flavor" of the church. Just as the minister is responsible for the type of ministry presented, the members are responsible for the kind of church they will have. It is not the minister that makes it a friendly church; it is the members. It is not the minister that determines the quality of ministry to the body; it is the members. Ushers, greeters, children's church workers, grounds keepers, teen leaders and all the other areas of helps ministry are made up of the members. The members in these ministries have the most direct contact with the people.

If you go to McDonald's tomorrow to buy a hamburger, it will not be the members of the board that will decide how you feel about McDonald's. It will not be a stockholder that cooks and determines the taste of your food. Your entire view of McDonald's multibillion dollar corporation is decided by the lowest man on the totem pole. The friendliness, quality of food, and overall perception of this multibillion dollar corporation will be determined by a minimum wage worker. If that person, who meets the public on the most basic level, fails to do his job properly, all else is of little value.

It is not the pastor that makes people feel welcome; all statistics show that it is the friendliness of the people. Less than 10% of the people in churches today are there because of the pastor. 70-90% of the people in churches today are there because of the influence of a friend or relative. An unfriendly church has unfriendly members. Unfriendly members make an unfriendly church, regardless of the minister.

Statistics also show that people stay in churches for social reasons more than anything else. It is rarely the minister that determines if people will stay in a church; it is the meaningful friendships they establish. One night I was invited to have dinner with a couple who had been attending my church. After dinner they announced that they were leaving the church. Then they spent at least ten minutes telling me how wonderful the ministry was at our church. They said, "Your ministry has affected our lives more than anything we've ever heard. Because of you, our children are serving God. We have never been anyplace that the praise and worship was as good." After several minutes, I finally interrupted, "If everything is so great, why are you leaving?" They said, "We don't have any friends there. We want to be somewhere where we have more in common with the people." It was not the quality of ministry that affected them in a negative way; it was the quality of friendships.

Many times I have had people who received phenomenal miracles, drastic life-changing events, powerful deliverance and still they would not stay in the church. In every case, they expressed the need to have more ministry for their children or more people their own age, in short, they wanted more of their social needs met. The minister cannot meet those needs; only the members can meet those needs.

Because some ministers have mistakenly believed and conveyed that the church was built on them, the people would blame them every time someone left. No doubt people do leave churches because of a negative experience with the minister, but if that person has meaningful relationships in the church, they will usually work through their problems with the minister. Most people are not willing to break their social ties because of a singular problem with a minister.

In the quest for control, both groups blame the other for people not staying in the church. The minister wants to appear right in the eyes of the people; the people want to avoid responsibility. Meanwhile, the world is going to hell and people's lives are being shattered, but we are too busy placing blame to deal with the real issues.

Each party must free the other to fulfill their role in the church. This will only happen as each party assumes responsibility. The minister should present the Word in a way that will meet the needs of the people. He should hear what the people say. He must be in touch with their needs. He must help organize areas of ministry to meet those needs. The member must assume responsibility for the quality of "body" ministry that will take place. Both parties should have respect and value for the other. Placing blame should not be the priority of either group; helping people should be the primary goal.

Because I have only pioneered churches, I have faced this dilemma more than once. A new church does not have the number of people to establish all the needed programs right from the start. In a new church, people come and love the ministry of the Word, but few stay and assume responsibility to help the church become what it ultimately will be. This is a perfect example of people not assuming personal responsibility.

When you find a church that has good ministry of the Word, before you leave because of a lack of "body" ministry, you should consider what your role in the church may be. If you recognize a need, maybe you are the one to do something about it. You may be the person the church needs to establish new areas of ministry. If there is a good Word and the pastor gives you the freedom to serve, you then become a key part in building the church.

When you go to a church that has a good ministry of the Word, yet is not very friendly, maybe you should be the one who breeds friendliness. Someone must be the initiator. That someone may be you. One person who assumes responsibility about a need will accomplish more than a thousand people who criticize a need. I have often seen entire churches change because of one person who sets the pace. I have seen churches become more friendly, more evangelistic, and more free in worship as the result of one individual who follows their heart.

It is so rare to find a church with the combination of a good Word and absence of control-oriented ministry. When you do, do not take it lightly. If there are needs you can meet, you may be the one who causes that church to grow and flourish. When someone sees a need, it is very possible that God is raising that person up to meet the need.

Chapter 12

What I Expect from My Pastor

We cannot live without hope (confident expectation). Faith springs from the root of hope. While it is essential to have hope (expectancy), this is also a major source of disappointment. *"Hope deferred maketh the heart sick: but when the desire cometh, it is a tree of life."* Proverbs 13:12. Expectations placed on others are probably our greatest source of disappointment. Our paradigms of "how things should be" create the basis for most of our frustrations and disappointments.

When we enter a relationship with a concept of how it should be (according to our paradigm), we have cheated the other person out of the opportunity to be him/herself. We enter the relationship demanding that the person be whom we want them to be. We reject them before we ever know them—and we cheat ourselves out of the opportunity of knowing and experiencing other people.

The seeds of destruction are always present at the beginning of any relationship. Most times, the destruction of a relationship is the product of unjust expectations. Any expectation that we place on another is unjust unless they have committed to fulfill those expectations. We should hear how that person plans to relate, decide if we can function within that environment, and then we can know what to expect. To assume that we know how a relationship will develop, or to expect it to develop a certain way, is the epitome of rejection, control, and domination.

Every person has an expectation of how a pastor should be. We think the pastor should visit everyone in the church, do hospital visitation, chair every committee and be present at every function. It has been these expectations that have driven ministers out of the ministry. It has prevented them from ever fulfilling their call. Worst of all, it has kept the members of the body from rising to their place of ministry. The minister has been the "paid professional" that has replaced the ministry of the member for far too many years.

Among many other variables, the Bible teaches that there are differences of administration. In other words, ten people could flow in the same gift or the same office and each of them would function differently. There is not a right or wrong way, unless a particular method directly opposes scripture. There is the way that works for the individual. Thus, every pastor will function differently. He will find a style of ministry and a style of relating that fits his behavioral pattern, his gifting and his personal preference.

Then the pastor will build a ministry team around him that fills the gaps for his weaknesses and strengths. Some pastors really enjoy personal visiting. Their absence from the office requires that they have a strong administrator on staff to meet the needs. Another pastor may be a strong administrator and will devote much time to organization. His strength of administration will create a weakness in personal involvement; he will need others to do most of the counseling and visiting. Some ministers will have a strong ministry of prayer and the Word. This will usually demand more seclusion than required by the average minister.

The ministry style of the minister will determine what types of people he will need around him. It will create opportunities for the members to minister. A person who is strong on personal visiting will often find himself in a church where that is a weakness of the minister. The first response is one of criticism. The member must, however, realize that the minister's weakness in this area opens the door of opportunity for the member to find a place of meaningful service.

I live by the philosophy that the one who

sees the need, is the one who should do something about it. The energy that it takes to criticize and stir up discontentment is the same energy it would take to rise to the opportunity. If there is a need in your church and the minister is willing to allow you to meet that need, you have no one to criticize but yourself, because you are refusing to do the very thing that your pastor is failing to do.

Teams are built around strengths and weaknesses. The minister needs members who are comfortable and effective doing the things he cannot do well. If the whole body were an eye, we could not hear. If the whole body were an ear, we could not walk. Do not criticize the other parts of the body for not being like you. You just do what you do best. Don't do it for a position; don't wait on a title. Do it because you care about people.

Because our church is very active on a national and international level, I am unable to give myself to individual ministry as much as some other pastors. This does not mean that I do not care about the individual. It means I have to organize to make sure the individual needs are met. Because I care, I organize. Yet because of the particular call on my life, I will always spend as much time away from the local church as I spend with it.

Many people expect a lot of personal involvement with their minister. In some settings this is possible, in others it is impossible. The way one interprets this will determine the attitude that individual will have toward the minister. It is possible that you will never become intimately involved with your church leaders. Because of church and family responsibilities and a personal social life, the minister may not have the personal time or the desire to expand his social life. This is not personal rejection; it is simply a matter of time. If your expectancy is personal involvement, you will be very disappointed. You may even become critical and faultfinding.

The way the church has tried to relate to ministers has not really worked. The minister has suffered, his family life has suffered and often his walk with God has suffered. Unrealistic demands have been placed on the minister. He has been expected to be an administrator, preacher, evangelist, social director, and the personal contact for every need in the church. This concept violates the model of the church as a body. It violates the teaching that every member should do its part. It is unscriptural, unrealistic and emotionally destructive.

Over the years, I have known people who seriously felt that their tithe was payment for the minister to serve them in the way they expected. When the minister failed to meet their expectations, they withheld their finances. This is a very warped perspective. There are needs in our lives that can only be met by our family and friends.   The ministry is not a substitute for relationships. Ministers are not paid friends.

I recall a lady many years ago who faced a situation that required her hospitalization. She was not friendly. She had not made friends within the church. When she was hospitalized, no one in the church knew about it. She became very offended that no one visited her.

When I discovered that she was sick, I went to see her. She began to complain and criticize the people. As she began to express her expectations of the people and ministers, she was describing things that would normally have been done by family and friends. She made some indications that she expected a certain kind of treatment for her giving.

Her expectation of church was unrealistic. Her paradigm was not based on any scriptural reality. Her perspective guaranteed hurt feelings and bitterness. She expected the church to replace and meet the needs of family and friends. While the church is a family that attempts to meet many needs of an individual, there is no substitute for personal family and meaningful relationships.

In a very loving way, I explained to her that if she wanted to have friends, she must show herself friendly. For the first time in her life, she had to face the consequences of being an unfriendly person. She was in a time of need with no friends. Unfortunately, she wanted people to be kind to her out of Christian obligation. Her expectation of the people and of the ministry was unrealistic. I explained to her that we were not her paid friends. I told her that I would help her if she wanted to make friends, but she could not force or hire the church or me to be her friend.

The early church established deacons (servants) to take care of the daily needs of the people, so the ministers could give themselves to prayer and the ministry of the Word. If today's minister attempts to meet all the expectations of the members, there is no way he will have time for a prayer life. He will not walk into the pulpit with something fresh and vibrant each week. He will not have the mind of the Lord for the church.

Enter a relationship with your pastor much like you would anyone else. Allow him to tell you what his ministry style is. If you have needs that are not met, ask questions—don't make accusations. Find out what is available to meet the needs of the people, then see what your part of meeting those needs could be. Remember, your church's weakness could be your opportunity to serve.

Becoming part of a local church means you will accept the ministry style of the local minister. Like any relationship, you cannot enter it with the intention of changing the other person. Relationships are built upon the basis of acceptance, not change. If your pastor changed for you today, he would have to change for someone else tomorrow. Allow him to be who he is in Jesus and you may find that he will be more willing to allow you to be who **you** are in Jesus.

Chapter 13

Why Churches Die

We have all seen it: churches that begin like a flame, only to burn out and become cold, dead, and lifeless. What happens in these churches? Is it some secret sin on the part of leadership? Is there some demon that steals away the life from the church? Is there some diabolical force that has crept in and stolen the life from the people?

While these are certainly possibilities, they are rarely the case. The members are always quick to want to find a mystical cause or someone to blame when there is no life. But remember, the church is people. The church is not the leadership. The church is not the organization. The church is the people—the members. Therefore for a church to die, something has to die in the people.

The truth is, churches die one member at a time. A person who is alive to God can feel and experience the presence of God anywhere. Paul and Silas were locked up in a dungeon. Their hands and feet were in stocks. They had no way to get comfortable. They could not even relieve themselves except on their own body. There was no one else in the prison that knew God. They were hated and the next day they would probably be put to death. It was as negative as any situation could be. Yet, they experienced God.

In the middle of the night, while others cried and complained, they worshiped God. In fact, they had a move of God that affected every other person in the place. They experienced God in a way that caused the salvation of everyone involved. You see, each person experiences God for themselves. The action of the group is never the final deciding factor as to whether or not you will experience God. We may let the group affect us. They may stimulate or they may demotivate, but only *we* determine if we will experience God.

More than once, I have been in a service that was just mediocre. Then some individual who was really experiencing something with God would prophesy, share a scripture, or just begin to freely worship. The actions of that one individual would often stimulate everyone in the place. Before long, there was an outbreak. It seemed as if someone opened a window and finally allowed God into the service. If that one individual had not moved ahead in what God was doing in them, everyone would have left the service saying, "God wasn't in that place today."

The truth is, God was always present, but the people were not responding to God and His goodness. They were responding to how they felt, the room temperature, or the uncomfortable seating. God did not arrive at the church service 35 minutes late because He was busy "pumping up" other churches. He was always there.

Unfortunately, our concepts of experiencing God are quite Old Testament. One of the phrases we often hear is "Enter into His presence!" We are always trying to get people to find and enter into the presence of God. We enter His gates with thanksgiving; we enter His courts with praise. If we will just do enough thanking and praising, we will enter in. While this is scriptural, it is the description of a person entering into the tabernacle of the *Old* Covenant to find and experience some degree of God's presence. This is *not* the description of a person who is born again and inhabited by the Spirit of the Living God.

There is really no such thing as a New Testament believer entering into the presence of God. He is with us and in us. We never leave the presence of the Lord. There is, however, the matter of how we are responding to the presence of the Lord. God is always good. He is always pouring out His blessings. Every day we are loaded with benefits. If we are aware of, sensitive to, and thankful for those benefits, we will respond to God and experience His presence. When people respond to what God has done and is doing, they experience something real with God.

In the Old Covenant, when God could not inhabit people, He inhabited buildings, temples, and tabernacles. He manifested Himself in the presence of the people in many ways. A common scripture we quote says, *"But thou art holy, O thou that inhabitest the praises of Israel."* Psalms 22:3. One translation says, *"God is enthroned on the praises of Israel."*

It may be true that God inhabited the praise of Israel, but today He inhabits His people. When we begin to acknowledge His goodness and His love, we enthrone Him. When we exalt Him, He becomes magnified in our midst instead of our problems and discomforts. Because we magnify Him, we begin to experience Him.

This does not have to be a random chance occurrence. It can happen any time people, individually or corporately, acknowledge God. He desires to show Himself strong. He desires to teach us, guide us, comfort us, and meet our every need. When He is not manifest in our presence, it is simply because of where our hearts are.

In my opinion, a lack of thankfulness is the first indication that we are backsliding. (My definition of backsliding is any form of going back in our relationship with God.) We backslide when we lose an awareness of God in our lives. When we are first saved, thankfulness is a predominate emotion. Because we are aware of God's love and goodness, we are continually thankful. God never stops being good to us. He never changes, but we change. We stop being thankful for God and what He is doing for us. That lack of awareness gives way to apathy, hardness of heart, and a lackadaisical attitude.

It is very easy at this point, to try to replace a living relationship with religious experiences. We start looking to someone other than ourselves to put us back in touch with God. We expect someone else to get and keep us excited. We look to others to give us only what God Himself can give us.

God is a heart God. All that He does, He does in and through our hearts. He wants to work in us at the level of our deepest emotions and strongest urges. He wants there to be life in us, then there will be life around us. If there is never life around me, I must realize that I have lost touch with the life of God in me.

When we worship, it will not be the mere actions that bring about the reality of God's presence. There is nothing we can do that will make us aware of the presence of God unless it is done at a heart level. We must bring our motives, will, and emotions into the participation of the worship of God, or it will be meaningless. All that we do, we must do from our hearts or it is meaningless.

Churches die because individuals harden their hearts to God. We come together and sing songs that we have sung before, quote scriptures we have quoted before, do the same things we've done thousands of times. But because we do not do these things from our hearts, all we experience is the boredom of the routine.

I have been in meetings where people were singing 400-year-old hymns and there would be freshness. It was as if they were singing them for the first time. I have also been where people were singing simple choruses with only two lines and they would sing those same two lines for what seemed like two hundred times, yet there would be excitement. These people were involving their hearts. It was real because it is real in their hearts.

The truth is, people who have life in their hearts, have life in their church. People who do not have life in their hearts could die of thirst in the middle of an oasis. A dead church is like a mirror held in front of the congregation.

When groups of individuals stop joyfully, thankfully responding to God, we have a dead church. There is nothing a preacher can do to cause a *move of God.* God is always moving. The question is "Am I moving with Him?" If I move, maybe others will follow. If I refuse to move and express what is in my heart because of others, then I, too, have become a contribution to the death of my church.

I must plan to be a part of the life of my

church. I must prepare for the services by doing some practical things: get a good night's rest, get up early so I can be there on time, avoid conflicts before church and come into the service ready to respond. It is amazing how punctuality affects a service. It affects me, as well as others. When I am late, I am not able to flow with the direction of the service. I just wander in and am only able to be an observer. I do not know what has happened. I have missed specific direction from the Holy Spirit. How I benefit from and contribute to a service is nearly always limited when I am late.

My tardiness has also had a negative affect on others. When others arrive promptly and the praise starts, they look around at the number of people who are absent and begin to question "What is wrong? Where is everyone?" Often this is when people become demotivated about their local church.

Then there are the leaders who have worked, prayed, and prepared. Often, this is why leaders get angry or feel unappreciated. They have prepared this service for you. They cannot understand why you have no value for what they have done. They want to help you, but you are not there. Often, the Holy Spirit will move powerfully with a *word* or a specific direction. It is sad when those who could be helped come in twenty minutes after it has all happened.

Pray before a service, see if God will give *you* a word or direction that will be a help to the service. You plan to have life, despite what anyone else does. If you bring the light, the light will always overcome the darkness.

Chapter 14

Family or Friends

Among the many misconceptions we have about church, I think there is no doubt a great misunderstanding about the type of relationship one is seeking to establish. There are many different levels of relating to a church, just as there are different levels of relating to people. It is essential that you understand how you want to relate to the church and how you expect the church to relate to you.

Many people want to relate to a church much the same as an immature young man wants to relate to a woman. He wants to receive the benefits of a committed relationship without making any commitments. Jesus taught about reciprocation in life, especially in relationships. In Luke 6:38, Jesus taught this important principle, *"Give, and it shall be given unto you; good measure, pressed down, and shaken together, and running over, shall men give into your bosom. For with the same measure that ye mete withal it shall be measured to you again."*

Unfortunately, this verse is usually taken out of context and used to teach about giving. While the principle of giving certainly applies, this verse is not talking about the giving of finances. It is talking about what we give to other people, i.e., mercy, love, judgment, etc. This verse describes what we should expect to receive from people based on what we give. We cannot receive from others what we are not willing to give. Right or wrong, people will respond to us, somewhat based on how we relate to them.

In a day when there has been so much abuse by church leaders, people have come to believe that commitment is a "four letter word." Commitment is actually a very essential part of mature life. But, commitment should never go beyond the bounds of personal choice. Commitment is always a matter of choice. It should never be forced or coerced. If it is, it is no longer commitment and it is no longer healthy.

Commitment can be perverted by the leader **or** the follower. The leader that attempts to demand commitment is not a leader. He is a dictator who is trying to force his views and goals onto others. He justifies his manipulation by his cause. Co-dependent people overcommit out of unhealthy motives. They, too, seek to use others to meet their own personal needs. Their commitment is really a means of manipulation. It is a way to force a person into a desired response. Then there are self-centered people who refuse to commit. Like all the others, they are also attempting to use other people for their own purposes.

Unfortunately, these people have so perverted the concepts of commitment that we have distorted paradigms concerning something that should be normal and healthy. We cannot look at all the abuses to determine how we feel about anything. We should return to the God-given principles involved and make decisions based on truth. There are people who eat until they become grossly overweight and die of heart disease, but that has never stopped me from eating. I need to eat to live and be healthy. Likewise, I need to be able to have healthy commitments, despite the abuses.

Without commitment, no marriages could last. There could be no jobs, no friends. Children would grow up without parents. The world, as we know it, cannot exist without people who are committed to certain things. There could be nothing of value in this life without commitment. It is this absence of healthy commitment that has robbed us of what were once common enjoyments of life, family and relationships.

We would not even have salvation if Jesus had not been committed. God called Jesus to a very difficult task. It was hard, painful and essentially unfair. Yet, out of His love for God and humankind, Jesus made a commitment that caused the salvation of all who would believe.

Commitment can only be made and understood by emotionally healthy people. Yet one can only become emotionally healthy as they make and maintain commitments. It is a successive process in which we grow in our ability to make commitments. As we experience the freedom and joy that come from those commitments, we grow in our ability to make and keep other, more demanding commitments.

Remember, we are not talking about toxic, controlling situations where one person dominates another. Neither are we talking about a dependency that is possessive and unrealistic. We are talking about a commitment to love one another and share the common burdens and responsibilities of a family—the body of Christ.

We cannot receive from others what we are unwilling or unable to give. Even if others attempt to give us what we will not give, we are emotionally incapable of receiving. God put this capacity in us at creation. We are created to be relationship-oriented people who live to give. We were created in the likeness and image of God. God, more than anything else, is love. It is always the nature of love to give. As we accept our identity in Him, giving will be a major part of what develops in us. First and foremost will be the giving of ourselves, then we will freely give of our resources.

When we first go to a church, we are usually going to receive. We are looking for what they can do for us. That is not entirely wrong.

We should properly evaluate any church before we make any commitments. We should know that we and our families will receive adequate ministry before we put down roots. Immature people tend to commit to things without really knowing the cost. Jesus said to always count the cost. You cannot count the cost if you do not know the cost.

One can remain a visitor at a church as long as is necessary before becoming a committed part of that local body. But you must realize that there will be much lacking in the relationship if you attempt to remain in the receiving phase forever. There will always be something that lacks in your heart's experience.

I have had people come to me and moan, "Pastor, I just don't feel like a part of things." Often, all I could say is, "Well, you really aren't a part of things. You are not involved. You come, receive and leave. That's like having sex with a hooker. There will never be any sense of relationship where there are not reciprocal commitments. Although you have been attending here for some time, you still relate to us like a friend instead of a family member."

There are many people who have never understood the difference between being a visitor and being a member. I liken it to friends or family members. Friends will do a lot for you. Friends will help when you are down. They are important and vital, yet there is something one shares from the heart with family that is never experienced with friends.

There are phases one goes through in relating to a church. Any of these phases may be bypassed based on your condition when you arrive. They may also exist simultaneously. There is that time, however, when your main goal is to receive help, the "*let us make you whole*" phase.

Next is the *member* phase. This is where one leaves the realm of just receiving and wants to become a responsible member of the family. There is security in having a family, a sense of belonging. There is something that cannot be experienced by an outsider. But even in a family, there are those who don't feel like they belong. They are usually the ones who do not assume their role and responsibility within the family. Every family member has responsibility.

In the Book of Galatians, Paul explained that we were no more servants, but sons. By being free from the law, we are free from the servant mentality that has to earn his place. The servant is never secure. His position is always determined by the quality of his work. It is actually a tormenting position.

Jesus brought us into the family. Through Him, we were adopted into the family. Our position is secure. We never serve to earn a position. We never serve to find a sense of security. When one crosses this line in his heart, life can become quite confusing. This is the realm of dead works. Only the righteousness that is given freely in Jesus can make us feel secure in God.

However, being a family member does not bring less responsibility; it brings more. The sense of ownership will always produce higher levels of commitment. I have owned my own businesses for most of my life. I assure you, when it's your business; you do not quit working just because it's four o'clock. You quit when the job is done. Long after the employees have gone home, the owner will still be working.

Similarly, long after friends have forgotten about your needs, the family will still be there taking care of you. Many people spend their entire lives away from their families. In the end, in the last hours, it's the family—not friends, who are there all night long. It's the family that pays the bills, not the friends.

When we become a part of the family, we receive a deeper sense of belonging. We come to a place where we have a sense of "ownership" in our local church. We feel like a part of things. We share the deeper joys with those who are family. Simultaneously, we receive a deeper sense of commitment. We accept our responsibilities in the family. We do our part; we carry our load. We experience the freedom that comes from giving of ourselves. We start experiencing what, until now, we have only heard about.

Personally, I think any person is not really a member (at a heart level) of a church until they have committed to carry their part of the load. Every person should be a giver and every person should be a minister. Until this is the level of your commitment, your heart will never allow you to taste a certain aspect of God. In this phase, one accepts the responsibility of giving, serving and helping the church as a whole to accomplish its mission.

To gain anything, we give up other things. To have a healthy marriage, two people give up certain freedoms. The freedoms that are normal when single would be destructive to a marriage. Only an extremely selfish person expects to be married and have all the freedoms of a single person.

To have children one must give up certain freedoms. The demands of raising a child do not allow one to have certain freedoms. Marriage does not *take* those freedoms from you; having children does not *take* those freedoms from you. You choose to *give* those freedoms to obtain these relationships.

In our relationship with a church, we will give up certain freedoms to gain other freedoms.

If we cling to one, we will despise the other.

If we want a sense of belonging, the feeling of purpose and productivity that comes from a healthy relationship with a church, we must be willing to assume the responsibilities of a family member.

Chapter 15

Becoming a Church Member

Becoming a member of a church means we are joining with a group of people for the benefit of everyone involved. We want our needs to be met. We want to learn and grow, but we must also bring our gifts, strengths, talents and resources to the group for the good of all. A church relationship can never be one-sided. Commitments should be reciprocal. We should recognize our need to give and receive.

One question people ponder about becoming a member of a church is in the area of finances. There is much debate about the tithe. With all that is said about the tithe, there is one issue that we must understand. God is logical. I do not think He selected 10% simply because it sounded good. I believe the 10% figure is based on some very sound, mathematical principles. It takes each person giving 10% of their income for the ministry to be able to adequately meet the needs of the people.

The more people a church has, the more needs it has. It needs an adequate building; it needs chairs, heating, offices. As a church grows, it needs a full-time pastor and maybe a youth pastor and materials for children's church. The expenses for this growth are only met when every member does his part. Whatever you believe about the theological aspect of tithing, the truth is: there cannot be effective ministry if people do not give at least 10% of their income.

In the Old Testament, when people brought their gifts to the priests, it met two needs. First, it provided for the needs of the priesthood. Ministers can only be available to minister when people give responsibly. Secondly, the people actually sat and ate part of their sacrifices. In other words, they partook of and benefited from the gift they brought to God. Similarly, we benefit from our giving to a local church.

When we give, we expand the quality of the ministry we receive. We insure the quality of ministry that our children receive, the comfort of our facility, and the availability of those who will minister to us. We, like the Old Testament believers, partake of the gifts we bring.

If every church member gave 10% of their income to the church, there would never be a need for special offerings. Ministers would not pressure people into giving. If every church member gave, the quality of ministry in every church would be at the level needed to sustain effective ministry to its own people.

Because we are emotional, social beings, it is essential that we establish meaningful relationships in our church. When we become a member of a church, we should take it upon ourselves to make friends. Our social needs must be met for us to stay in a church. Unless we are involved socially, we will never feel we are a part. Despite how valuable the ministry may be, we will not stay in a church that does not meet our social needs.

To a limited degree, a church can establish programs that facilitate involvement with others. This seldom meets our social needs. Whatever the programs, we should seek out and develop new friendships. The Bible says it like this, *"A man that hath friends must show himself friendly: and there is a friend that sticketh closer than a brother."* Proverbs 18:24. We should initiate finding friends. We should not expect others to seek us out.

It is also important that we find a place to serve. Many important needs in our life are only met as we serve others. A failure to become a part of the team will translate into a failure to feel like part of the team. People who are involved in serving do not earn the acceptance of the church leaders, but because they are involved with the leaders regularly, this becomes a means of establishing relationships with those in leadership. As we serve, we will also deepen our realization of Christ in us. We will benefit personally from pouring our lives out. In Philemon 6, the New International Version reads, "*I pray that you may be active in sharing your faith, so that you will have a full understanding of every good thing we have in Christ.*" You, more than anyone else, will benefit as you minister and meet the needs of others.

If you are not ready to be involved in ministry of the Word, become a part of the helps ministry. The helps ministry is essential for a church to function. It may not get the same public attention as the ministry of the Word, but one cannot survive without the other. The helps ministry makes it possible to present the Word of God unhindered. When the practical needs are met, the minister of the Word has the freedom to focus in on ministry. Deacons, which are actually servants, met several needs in the early church. Not only did they meet the practical needs of the people, they expanded the ministry of the Word of God.

"*Then the twelve called the multitude of the disciples unto them, and said, It is not reason that we should leave the word of God, and serve tables.*" Acts 6:2. Those who preach the Word need and rely on those who minister to all the practical needs. If the minister of the Word is encumbered with other areas of the ministry, he will be unable to give himself to his calling. This does not free him from service. He is simply able to focus on his area of serving. *"But we will give ourselves continually to prayer, and to the ministry of the word."* Acts 6:4.

Unfortunately, those who minister in the more practical areas often fail to see their real value to their ministry. They do not understand that clean nurseries promote trust in parents who need to be in the service hearing the Word. We often fail to realize that a clean building and grounds cause people to have a positive evaluation of our ministry. Ushers and greeters make people feel welcome. Musicians stimulate people to praise and worship. Sound people make the sound pleasant. Janitors, painters, carpenters and a thousand other people are part of having effective Sunday morning worship services. When everyone does their part, it has the same effect as it did in the Book of Acts. *"And the word of God increased; and the number of the disciples multiplied in Jerusalem greatly . . . "* Acts 6:7.

When you are attracted to a church, do not bring all of your old paradigms with you. Before you try to make your new church conform to your ideas, see how it is working. We often treat our churches much like we treat our spouses. We fall in love, we get married, then we try to make them change. Often, we destroy our relationship with a healthy church because we want to make it fit our paradigm. Give it a chance. After all, if what you had was all that good, you would not have changed churches. If you had not seen something you liked, you would not have joined this church.

Being part of any group: marriage, family, business, friendship, or church means commitment. It does not just mean commitment to the group, but also commitment to the principles involved with having relationships. It means commitment to the things that make a relationship healthy and positive. Relationships are impossible without commitment. Above all, a commitment to the church is a part of and an expression of our commitment to the Lordship of Jesus.

Chapter 16

How to Leave a Church

I realize that it is often hard to find a church that is healthy. Many people across the country are in a church dilemma. Often a person has been hurt so deeply they are afraid to trust again, or because of emotional problems, keep being attracted to unhealthy situations. For you, all I can say is this, "Find a church that is strong on the love of God." Even if they do not believe the things you believe, you should be safe.

Find a pastor who is a kind, loving individual. Look at how he relates to his family. That is the reality, not his pulpit ministry. Under the list of qualifications for elders, it has more to do with his daily life than it does his ministerial life. A kind individual who does not have a great amount of revelation can bring more healing into your life than a "spiritual giant" who does not walk in love.

All of the things we do in our relationship with a church are an expression of our relationship with Jesus. Even if someone used you, you have still done what you did "unto the Lord." Like Jesus, we must commit ourselves to the One who judges faithfully. Some pastor may have used us and then rejected us, but Jesus sees our labors of love as a sweet smelling sacrifice.

The Apostle Paul, before his conversion, learned an important truth: what you do to the church, you do to Jesus, Himself. The early church was not flawless. It certainly had its problems, but it was still the body of Christ. When Paul afflicted the church Jesus met him and asked, *"Why are you persecuting me?"* Paul never realized that what he did to the church he did to Jesus. We should never treat the church any differently than we would treat Jesus.

You may see things in a particular church that you dislike. You may hear doctrines with which you disagree. You may even have a negative experience with a leader. If these things happen, never lose sight that you are still dealing with the body of Christ.

If the time comes that you want to change churches, do it in a way that is healthy. You do not need to justify your decision by finding fault with the church. Do not destroy the confidence that others have in a church simply because you have lost your confidence. Too often we want others to feel about things the way we feel. In an attempt to create this, we often destroy innocent people.

If you leave a church, walk in love. Appreciate what you have received. Remember the value that has come into your life through that ministry. Accept your responsibility for any unhealthy relationships and walk away. Maintain peace in your heart, despite how they react to you.

Do not judge the next church by the one you left. There are good churches and there are good men and women of God out there. You can be blessed if you do not destroy your heart with bitterness. Do not let a corrupt church cause you to become incapable of benefiting from a good church.

Allow your integrity to be the product of how Jesus has treated you, not how a person has treated you. Jesus has never hurt you. He has not abused you. He has never used you. He has never rejected you. If His body is weak and sickly, the last thing it needs is a few more stripes.

If you feel you should leave your present church, walk away in love. If you abuse them for abusing you, you are no different from them.

If you allow yourself to become bitter, it will destroy your future relationships with other churches. Do all you can to maintain peace.

You do not need to go to your pastor and tell him all you dislike. After all, you probably gained some good things while you were there. Why not send him a note thanking him for all the good things you received and let him know you are withdrawing membership.

Do not be drawn into contentions. If you have decided to leave, there is no need for an official meeting where you run the risk of hurt feelings on both sides.

Do not stay out of church. Look around, visit and ask questions. Take the time to find a church where you can put down roots and pursue your dreams. You can have a healthy relationship with a church, regardless of their motives. In a good church relationship, you will find satisfaction for your soul.

When you go to another church, do not join right away. Get to know the people. Meet and observe the personal lives of the leaders. Do not make the same mistakes as before.

Chapter 17

Overcoming Offense

It would be wonderful to think that the church and Christian fellowship could be a place where there would never be offense, to even wish for that in this life is, at best, idealistic. Where there are people, there will be offense—but offense does not have to end in destruction, rejection and years of complex, emotional problems.

The only reason that offenses have such a dramatic effect on us is that we, in our unbelief, try to deal with offense unscripturally. There is actually nothing that anyone does that can destroy you unless you handle it in an unscriptural manner. When we reject Jesus' teaching and opt for our own opinions and views, we have excluded God and His healing power from that part of our lives. We are limited to our own resources.

Every offense that comes our way has the potential to destroy us. It is not, however, the offense itself that contains this power. The potential for destruction lies in how we handle offense. In Luke 17:1, Jesus made it as plain as it can be, *"It is **impossible** but that offense will come . . ."* If Jesus said it was impossible for it to be any other way, one would think that we would prepare a little better for it. Jesus went on to explain the difficulties for those who become the source of offense. But then, in verse 3, He focuses the emphasis back on us, *"Take heed to yourselves: If thy brother trespass against thee, rebuke him; and if he repent, forgive him."* Luke 17:3. "Why should I take heed if my brother offends me? He's the one with the problem. He is the one who committed the sin." This may be true, but it is actually easier for him to deal with his part of this than it is for me to deal with my part.

If he offended me, he has no excuse. His part is really clear cut, but my part is not so clear. I can now justify all manners of sin because of the way he treated me. Now that I have an excuse, I think I can sin and it will not affect me—but it will. Sin will kill me whether I do or do not have an excuse.

Jesus said there is only one way to deal with offense when it comes, "Forgive them!" At this, the apostles said "Increase our faith!" In other words, it is going to take a lot of faith to do this. This is something great. This is far above and beyond the norm for the Christian. It is really going to take some special anointing to be able to forgive the one who offends me. Jesus' reply about the sycamine tree was actually a rebuke. It only takes a grain of faith to make a tree be uprooted and cast into the sea. Forgiving people is never a problem of faith; it is a problem of choice.

We hold onto offense so we will have a basis for harboring sin. Offenses justify our gossiping, backbiting and passing judgment. We use them to justify our sinful attitudes and actions. Failure to forgive is a choice. We fail to see the destruction of sin, because we want to get in the last word, because we desire to make someone else suffer or make them pay; we choose to hold our offense. In so doing, we always destroy ourselves more than we destroy them.

Jesus tells about a servant who worked all day in the field. When he came in from the field, he prepared his master's food. He went without until his master was provided for. After the master had eaten then the servant was allowed to eat. In so doing, he had done nothing more than his natural responsibility. In light of what we have been forgiven, to hold unforgiveness in our hearts for anything would be completely and utterly foolish. It should be natural to forgive any offense.

It may even be valuable, at this point, to understand what an offense is. Our modern concept of an offense is anything that another does that hurts my feelings or makes me feel bad. That is hardly the case. The New Testament definition of offense is *to lay a snare or a trap that causes one to fall or be drawn into sin.*

Many people become offended at the truth. Jesus, Himself, is the rock of offense. Many people are offended by correction. The correction they consider an offense is not a snare to draw them into sin, it is something to draw them out of the sin they were in.

When Christians who are in sin become offended it is because they are not receiving truth. They intend to stay in that sin. They are "offended" because their deeds have been exposed. This is where real destruction starts. When someone who is in sin rejects counsel, they will seek to justify themselves by drawing others into that conflict. They want others on their side. They want the security found in numbers. Therefore, they tell others about how someone hurt them. They will repeat the story in a way that emphasizes their hurt. They may even tell the truth about what the other person said or did to them, but what they will never tell you is the sin they were in. They will never tell you the truth about why they were offended.

In actuality, even though this person was hurt by some confrontation, they did not experience what the Bible calls an offense. They experienced the love of someone who cared enough to confront them about their destructive lifestyle. Because they intended to stay in sin, they responded in a negative way. Now they are the ones who are creating the offense. They are the one's who are drawing others into sin. They are drawing others into a trap of destruction.

It all seems so innocent. We are just allowing someone to share their hurts with us. We are just lending an ear. We are just being there for a friend. The problem is, however, now we are offended. We are angry. There is a breach in our relationship with someone who is not even there to defend himself. Unfortunately, this will happen more concerning ministers and leaders than it will anyone else.

Ministers and leaders are very easy targets. We continually deal with people who have deep emotional problems. We deal with people who are in sin. We deal with the most intimate and difficult areas of a person's life. Because of that, we are the focus of much of their anger and frustration. When a person decides to rebel, get into sin, leave church or do anything unscriptural, they must have a way to justify it in their own hearts. More times than not, a church leader will be the focus of that justification.

When a person destroys our confidence in church leaders, it is never as innocent as it seems. It is rarely a matter of one person sharing their hurt with another. There is usually an agenda. That agenda is the attempt to try to draw you into my offense. I want you to feel about someone the way I feel. I want you to be on my side. I want vindication by your approval of my actions. I want you to tell me it is all right to have sinful attitudes and actions. The Book of Proverbs explains the motives of the talebearer. No matter how fair it sounds, there is really hatred at the root of his talebearing. *"He that hateth dissembleth with his lips, and layeth up deceit within him; When he speaketh fair, believe him not: for there are seven abominations in his heart."* Proverbs 26:24-25.

We should always beware of the talebearer. Despite how dear a friend, no matter how kind a person, whatever we think, hatred is their motive. They are willing to sacrifice your peace and your relationships on the altar of their hatred. And we are like sheep led to the slaughter. Because we do not believe and observe God's Word in the area of communication and relationships, we stroll blindly into the trap. Then we cannot understand why we have bitterness and hatred in us. We cannot understand why we have lost relationships that have been meaningful to us in the past.

Again, Proverbs explains what happens, *"The words of a talebearer are as wounds, and they go down into the innermost parts of the belly."* Proverbs 26:22. Something gets wounded in us when we listen to the talebearer. Something in our heart changes. We cannot love and trust in the same way we previously could.

This is where we have to assume

responsibility. If I were not involved in the sin of gossip, I would not have destroyed my heart in this area. Passively listening to slanderous gossip is just as much sin as speaking slanderous gossip. One must be realistic about one's ability to recover offended people.   Galatians 6:1 encourages us to help those who are overtaken, but it also gives us a warning, *"Brethren, if a man be overtaken in a fault, ye which are spiritual, restore such a one in the spirit of meekness; considering thyself, lest thou also be tempted."*

Do not try to be the restorer of discontented people if you cannot do so without falling into temptation yourself. The greatest temptation will be to accept the same unscriptural attitudes and actions as those who are offended. If you cannot handle it, stay out of it. Jesus warned us to do everything possible to protect ourselves from offense. Cut off your hand, pluck out your eye, whatever it takes. Do not let yourself take up an offense. Why? You might not recover. You never know what offense will destroy you. Eternal life, peace and joy are too valuable to risk with offenses, especially the offenses of others.

Where this really becomes utterly sinful is when we take up an offense against a leader. It is not a greater sin to slander a leader than it is to slander anyone else. The problem is, it has stronger, more devastating results. There is more at stake than the assumed "special status" of a minister when the Bible says, *"Touch not mine anointed, and do my prophets no harm."* Psalms 105:15.

When we sow mistrust for any leader, we are sowing mistrust for all leaders. The way a person views a leader has more potential for destruction than our view of another member. You will not leave church over the way you feel about a member, but you will leave church and God over the way you feel about a leader. The leader is no more special to God than you or anyone else. His position, though, is more weighty than the average Christian.

Charismatics are probably the worst about slandering leaders. Why? We expect more from our leaders. We expect them to solve our problems. When they do not, we slander them. Also, when a person leaves a denominational church, he will probably go to another denominational church in his city. He is not completely betraying those in his previous church. He is still a part of their denomination. Therefore, it is unlikely that he will hear criticism about his new church or new pastor. After all, that new church is a part of the same denomination as the church he left.

When you leave a charismatic or independent church there is more of a sense of betrayal to the leader. Therefore, there is more potential for hurt by the leader and the members. Even though you may go to another independent church, you are no longer a part of the same group. It is more likely that you will hear criticisms about the new church and pastor. People from your past church will slander your new church and leaders as a way to win back your confidence.

The problem, however, is that to undermine your confidence in one leader will automatically undermine your confidence in every leader, to some degree. By the time you have changed churches two or three times, you have heard so many rumors about all of your previous leaders, you do not trust anyone. The result— you leave church and backslide.

The Bible warns us about receiving a bad report against an elder. *"Against an elder receive not an accusation, but before two or three witnesses. Them that sin rebuke before all, that others also may fear."* 1 Timothy 5:20. When the scripture says to rebuke those who sin before everyone, it is talking about those who sin in this matter of receiving an evil report.

Does this mean it is all right for leaders to sin? No! Does this give leaders more privileges than anyone else? No! Does this mean leaders cannot be challenged? No! Because of the weight of our responsibility, we should walk as discretely as possible. When a leader sins, he can do much damage. Usually, however, there is more damage done by those who spread the evil report than there was by the sin of the leader. This strong admonition of publicly correcting those who bring and receive evil reports is because of the great destruction that comes about by this sin. Keep in mind, if you receive it (accept it as true), you will become a part of spreading it, whether covertly or overtly.

A person who is walking in love is always seeking restoration. If they want restoration, they will always go to the one with whom they have conflict. When they go to others, they have proven their destructive intentions. They want to destroy the one with whom they have conflict and they are willing to destroy you in the process. If you get involved, you become a willing participant in the destruction of your own heart. Proverbs describes it like this, *"He that passeth by, and meddleth with strife belonging not to him, is like one that taketh a dog by the ears."* Proverbs 26:17. The next time you get involved with discontentment that is not your own, just remember, you would be wiser to find a big, mean dog and grab him by the ears than you would be to get involved in strife that does not belong to you. The dog's bites will heal with time; the wounds of a talebearer may never heal.

The person who tells you his side first will always seem right. The fact that his story seems right to you, is an indicator of your lack of spiritual and scriptural insight. Of course it sounds right; you have not heard the other side of the story. *"He that is first in his own cause seemeth just; but his neighbour cometh and searcheth him."* Proverbs 18:17. A wise man, on the other hand, will not form an opinion until he has all the information. *"He that answereth a matter before he heareth it, it is folly and shame unto him."* Proverbs 18:13.

Just the fact that this person has involved me should tell me something. I may not know if what they are telling me is true, but I do know that they are in sin by trying to involve me. I do know that they are handling their problem from an unscriptural basis. They are in sin, so wisdom would dictate that I be very cautious of this person.

If I am not willing to help this person assume their responsibility to deal with this in a scriptural way and bring about restoration, then I am a part of their destruction. When I allow a person to give me a report about anyone, I am now a part of the problem. When I point them in a scriptural direction, I am now a part of the solution.

If I am to have peace and healthy relationships with my church I cannot be a willing participant in gossip, strife and discord. I cannot have healthy attitudes toward those about whom

I am gossiping. If I have something to work out with a leader, I should work it out with him. If someone else has something to work out with a leader I should encourage them to work it out with that person. Or, I may even need to go with them to work it out.

In this area I must heed what are some of the strongest warnings in the Bible. More than anything else, I do not want to affect a person's walk with God nor the body of Christ. We are the temple of God, i.e., we, plural, corporately. God lives in us individually, but together we are being built into the temple of God. *"Know ye not that ye are the temple of God, and that the Spirit of God dwelleth in you? If any man defile the temple of God, him shall God destroy; for the temple of God is holy, which temple ye are."* 1 Corinthians 3:17.

This is not a verse about murder or suicide. It is a verse about people who would defile, spoil, stain, make to wither, harm in any way the church. In this case, it was people who were arguing over which apostle was right. One went with this teacher; another went with that teacher. That would have been fine, but they drew others into it. They divided the church over this issue. God said that if you defile my church, you will be defiled. You will wither; you will be the one to suffer. I am not talking about God judging you, but this is a strong warning.

In 1 Corinthian 11:29 it describes people who are sick and dying because they fail to discern the body. People fail to discern the body of Christ that was broken on the cross. People also fail to discern the body of Christ that is here on the earth . . . the church. The Holy Spirit is in each of us, but together we become the temple of God. Like Paul learned on the road to Damascus, what we do to the church we do to Jesus. When we slander others, our tongues become whips that add lashes to the body of the Lord Jesus. We are no different from the Roman soldiers who whipped Jesus before His crucifixion. The body of Christ will always recover, but the individual who is discouraged by our slander may never recover.

Chapter 18

Determining Destiny

Among the many capacities that God gave man, the capacity for freedom has been the most powerful and far-reaching. In order for us to have the capacity for loving relationships, we must also have the capacity of choice, i.e., freedom. Along with the capacity for freedom and choice came personal responsibility. It is impossible to have freedom without having responsibility.

In irresponsible selfishness, we have wanted freedom apart from responsibility. We have wanted to be able to make our own choices and then blame God for the consequences of those choices. This is an age-old problem. One of the clearest places this is evident is in the Book of Job. Job made specific choices. His motives for making those decisions were good, but motive is not the qualifying factor for decision making. Many people with good motives have made decisions that were not based on God's Word. The consequences of those decisions were destruction. Millions of people have died because someone with a good motive made an unscriptural decision.

Job made decisions about how he would raise his children. His children were irresponsible in their relationships with God because of his choices. This caused Job to live in fear for their lives. Ultimately, they were all killed. Like millions of others, Job blamed this on God. (There is more perverted teaching twisted from the Book of Job than almost any other book of the Bible.) Job insisted that he was right. After all, his motives were right.

But Job didn't teach his children about God and godliness; he prayed for them. He wanted God to do for his children what he was unwilling to do for them. Job, not God, determined the destiny of his family. When disaster came, he did not want to accept any responsibility for that disaster.

Job tried to convince all of his friends that he was right. He went to great lengths to explain the cleanness of his hands. But in justifying himself, he automatically implicated God as the source of his family's problems. After chapters of arguing with his friends, God finally speaks. When God speaks, we have the only legitimate opportunity to extract doctrine from the Book of Job. *"Wilt thou also disannul my judgment? Wilt thou condemn me, that thou mayest be righteous?"* Job 40:8. Job's refusal to accept personal responsibility automatically condemned God as the guilty party.

The Book of Proverbs says it this way, *"The foolishness of man perverteth his way: and his heart fretteth against the LORD."* Proverbs 19:3. The Amplified Bible interprets *fretting against God* as blaming God. When we make unscriptural decisions, we will have to live with the consequences. However, we and others often blame God. I have met numerous people who would not get saved because they blamed God for all the hardship and suffering in the world. They ask, "Why doesn't God do something about it?" It seems like a reasonable question, but it is not!

   We cannot have it both ways. We cannot have freedom apart from responsibility. If God makes us free, it is impossible for Him to be responsible for what happens. God gave us His Word so we could know how to win in every situation. He gave us the ingredients, direction, and wisdom for a life that would be filled with peace and assure peace to future generations. If we want good consequences from our decisions, we must base those decisions in God's Word. Because we do not trust God, we choose to make decisions apart from the wisdom of His Word. We construct the snare for our destruction, as well as for destruction of future generations. We dig the ditch we will fall in. The Psalmist talks about the wicked man who does not honor God: *"He made a pit, and digged it, and is fallen into the ditch which he made."* Psalms 7:15.

   The condition of the world today is not the product of God's judgement against man; it is not the result of mystical decisions made from heaven. The condition of the world today is the result of the decisions that *men* have made. Men have progressively moved away from God. They often did not think they were, they had right motives, but you must remember, the Jews had good motives for crucifying Jesus, too. They did it in the name of God; they rejected the portion of the scripture that did not fit into their agenda. Similarly, we make decisions that we say are for the right reasons, yet if they have no basis in God's Word, we will suffer the consequences. In fact, if our decisions are not based on God's Word, we are either ignorant or working our own agenda.

God intended that planet Earth be a paradise. He created the world the way He wanted it in the beginning. When He placed Adam in the garden, He gave him authority—the right and freedom of choice. God would not *make* Adam do anything; he had the right to choose. Unfortunately, Adam used that right of choice in a destructive way. He had good motives and good logic. But despite the logical arguments and the fact that his wife was in agreement with the decision, the result was still the same—DEATH!

Adam's sin did not mean death for him alone. It also meant death for every person that would ever live. In other words, his decision affected unborn generations. Until this very day, Adam's decision affects every human being. You can say "That's not fair," but fair is not the issue here. Freedom is the issue. It may not be fair, but it was *his* choice. You cannot have it both ways; you will eat of the fruit of your decisions. Unfortunately, your children and your children's children will also eat of the fruit of your ways.

You might argue, "God should have done something." He did! He told Adam what he should do and the consequences that would come if he did something else. God has also told *us* what to do in His Word. He has told us the consequences of doing things another way. Will you use *your* freedom for life or death? When you experience destruction, remember it is your choice. *"I call heaven and earth to record this day against you, that I have set before you life and death, blessing and cursing:therefore choose life, that both thou and thy seed may live:"* Deuteronomy 30:19.

When we choose death, we never call it death. We call it preference, our right—and it is. But every choice that does not have its roots in truth, is a choice for death. God has set before us the way of life and the way of death. We will live with the fruit of our choices.

From the time of Adam until now, men have made decisions that moved future generations away from God. Stop and think about it. There was a time when every living, human being had the knowledge of God. But along the way, some people made decisions without qualification in God's Word. Those decisions, even though they may have been subtle and seemingly insignificant, have resulted in entire nations that reject God.

Curses that are passed down from generation to generation are not nearly as mystical as it might initially seem. When parents make decisions about anything, those decisions form the views of their children. If those decisions are unscriptural, the children learn to be godless. They, in turn, teach their children to be godless. Followers always take if further than leaders. Whatever the leader, parent, or one-in-charge does, the followers will go beyond that. They do not have the same reasoning and experience as the leader, therefore, they always go to greater degrees of boldness, honesty—or departing from God.

We all have a circle of influence. Like it or not, your decisions always affect others. No one ever goes astray alone. *"He is in the way of life that keepeth instruction: but he that refuseth reproof erreth."* Proverbs 10:17. The original language indicates that the one who *refuseth instruction* not only erreth, but he "causeth to err." In other words, when we will not be taught by God's Word, *we* not only err, but we also cause others to err.

Our circle of influence could involve many innocent victims, but the greatest tragedy of error is the effect it has on our children. In any way that we depart from truth, our children are watching, learning, evaluating, and duplicating. The sins of the parents nearly always become the sins of the children. Ironically, I have had hundreds and possibly thousands of parents sit across my desk seeking help for their children. I could not help the child, however, because of the parent. The message the parent was sending was stronger than anything I could say. After having a Christian school as a part of my ministry for a number of years, I saw that the only children I could not reach were the ones whose parents made it impossible.

Children copy their parents. The parents are the main source of developing attitudes and beliefs in a child. The attitudes and beliefs of the parents are duplicated, no, multiplied in the child. The sad fact is, children do not learn from what you say nearly as much as by what you do. They watch your actions and independently interpret them.

One situation in which many parents condemn future generations, is in their relationship with the local church. By observing *your* relationship with the church, your children evaluate your relationship with God. When you have no value for church, the child interprets that as no value for God. We all need functional ways to express and demonstrate our faith. How much more do children need something tangible to help them grasp the intangible?

God incorporated many *ceremonies* into Christianity as a way to help us grasp intangible realities. Baptism, for example, is a ceremony where we demonstrate faith in the fact that we have died with Christ and are raised up in newness of life. God, in His wisdom, knew that we needed something tangible as a way to express and grasp the intangible. Through the action of baptism we activate something in our heart that can cause us to grasp the reality of resurrected life.

Communion finds its meaning in these same principles. When we take communion, we exercise faith. We stir up in our hearts the realities that are being demonstrated by the bread and wine. There is something that should happen to us at a heart level as a result of what we are doing on a natural level. For this reason, we must always leave the realm of ceremony and enter the realm of faith. The way these things affect our heart is what gives them validity and purpose. God, in His wisdom, recognized that we needed to have natural, tangible ways to express, and thereby experience, our faith.

Church is much the same, although it has

a far wider scope of reality than any of these ceremonies. Apart from the meaningful participation in a local church, we tend to lose contact with the realities of God. We may continue reading our Bible and praying for a while, but ultimately we lose touch with many of the essentials of Christian life. The truth is: we may endure all of that, we may never attend church the rest of our lives and still maintain some spark of what we had with God—but our children will not.

A child who grows up outside of church will have little basis for God in his life. He will have no positive peer pressure. His scope of realization of godliness will be limited. Even if that child is able to grasp some diminished realities of God, his children will never see God. By our unscriptural actions of departing from the church, we determine the destiny of unborn generations.

I know of many situations where people left church angry and hurt. They had a bad experience that caused them to withdraw trust from leaders. While they could justify their hurt, they can never justify their unscriptural decisions and its effect on their children. I have seen entire families depart from God because their parents departed from church. If you talk to the parents, they will tell you they know God. They will still have a real profession of Jesus, but their children may have no relationship with God at all.

Being a vital part of a church *is* scriptural. It is something God tells us to do. That, alone, should be sufficient reason. But far beyond the issue of obedience, is the issue of destiny. What will be the destiny of future generations if we assume to be wiser than God? How will our children interpret our actions? How will their children be affected?

Everyone wants to be important. Well, you cannot get any more important than this. The wisdom of your decisions will determine the fate of future generations. Honor God in all your decisions and eat the fruit of godliness. Honor God in all your decisions and feed the children of the future from the Rivers of Life. Their destiny is in your hands!

Conclusion

We need the local church, just as we need one another. We will never be what we need to be and the world will never see what it needs to see, apart from a healthy, loving church.

By observing God's wisdom in relating to individuals, as well as to a church body, the local church will become a place of health and healing. We have the opportunity to be part of something bigger than ourselves, influence people, develop our gifts and calling, grow in worthwhile friendships, and have boundaries of acceptable behavior that serve as a warning when we err.

The church will never meet the idealistic expectations of co-dependent judgement, but neither will anyone nor anything for very long. For me, my relationship with the church has been over twenty years of friends, family, and fun. I don't want what the world has to offer. Neither do I want what is offered from the person who has rejected the church. It is not based on reality.

As I mentioned previously, many of those who were saved in the early days of the Jesus movement are no longer committed to the Lord. I do not know what was in their hearts or all the issues involved, but I do know that one common denominator among those who have fallen has been the rejection of the church.

When I was doing my undergraduate

work, I saw many students become angry at leadership for one thing or another. Sometimes it was justified; sometimes it was not. I saw idealism destroy many. Again, the common denominator was the rejection of the local church. Many of those students left in sin and rejected the local church to fellowship with the church "at large." Today, I can't find many of those people either.

In my nearly 20 years as a pastor, I have seen almost every imaginable scenario. I have seen people recover from nearly every kind of sin. Those who fall the farthest and are least likely to recover, are those who reject the fellowship of other Christians who *are* in a healthy relationship with a church.

Today, my dearest friends are people in the church. The people who challenge me are in the church. The people who have been a part of my life and my children's lives are in the church. Have I ever been hurt? "Sure I have!" But don't fool yourself, Christians are not the only ones who will hurt you. Anywhere there are relationships, there will be hurt. But we, the members of the body, have a common denominator that brings us together. We have a basis to resolve our conflict.

Ask God to heal you of the hurts and disappointments you have received from people in the church. Remember all the good things that have happened to you as a result of the church. Assume your responsibility in healthy relationships. Restore your walk with the church. Don't relate the way you did in the past. Do not be idealistic. Learn to be a friend and thereby develop meaningful friendships in a local church.

Our children, and most of the world, equate the church with God. Only idealism thinks that paradigm can be changed. Let's be a part of bringing healing to the church so our children, friends, and relatives will see the life and love of God in practice.

Let us insure that our church will be a place of healing. If they see us fight and slander one another, they will say we are no different from the world. But let the world see us love one another, and as they see us forgive and walk in love, they will surely want what we have.

The church is the family of God. This family relationship is expressed through the local church. Cause your church to be a loving family.